The River Cottage

Curing & Smoking Handbook

The River Cottage Curing & Smoking Handbook

by Steven Lamb

with an introduction by
Hugh Fearnley-Whittingstall

TEN SPEED PRESS
Berkeley

For Elli, Aggie & Betsy

Copyright © 2014 by Steven Lamb
Photography copyright © 2014 by Gavin Kingcome
Illustrations copyright © 2014 by Toby Atkins

Published in the United States by Ten Speed Press, an imprint of the
Crown Publishing Group, a division of Random House LLC,
a Penguin Random House Company, New York.
www.crownpublishing.com
www.tenspeed.com

Ten Speed Press and the Ten Speed Press colophon are registered
trademarks of Random House LLC.

Originally published in slightly different form in Great Britain
by Bloomsbury Publishing Plc, London, in 2014.

Library of Congress Cataloging-in-Publication Data
Lamb, Steven.
The River Cottage curing & smoking handbook / by Steven Lamb ;
with an introduction by Hugh Fearnley-Whittingstall.
pages cm
1. Cooking (Meat) 2. Cooking (Smoked foods) 3. Food—Drying.
4. Smoked foods. 5. River Cottage (Television program)
I. Title. II. Title: River Cottage curing and smoking handbook.
TX749.L227 2015
641.6'6—dc23
2014030671

ISBN 978-1-60774-787-1 (hardback) — ISBN 978-1-60774-788-8 (ebook)

Printed in China

Design by Will Webb

10 9 8 7 6 5 4 3 2 1

First United States Edition

Contents

Ever since I first embarked on my River Cottage adventures, almost two decades ago, I've had the same aim: to bring myself and, with luck, those around me closer to the source of what we eat. That might mean something as simple as buying eggs from a neighbor rather than a supermarket, or learning how to cut up a whole chicken rather than buying it in expensive portions. But I've derived huge pleasure and satisfaction from delving further into the realms of food production – growing my own vegetables, for instance, and raising my own livestock.

Such projects, though hugely enjoyable, are undeniably challenging and involve some commitment. I know they're not for everyone – or at least, not yet. But if you would like to give a bit less space to the middlemen and regain control, at least to some extent, over what you're feeding your family, then there are other elements of food production you can take into your own hands with amazing ease. Home curing and smoking are among the most enticing.

These are techniques that take you one delicious step beyond your average recipe. They represent a deeper level of engagement with food than baking a cake or simmering a stew – perhaps because they require the deployment of often ancient artisanal skills. These skills need not be daunting, but they do set you off on a new learning curve. The cook who makes his or her own bacon enters a different arena from the one who roasts his or her own pork. And, correspondingly, he or she reaches a new level of gratification – often by no means instant, but always lasting.

Having said that, many of Steven's fantastic recipes are very straightforward and relatively quick. These dishes do a great deal to dismantle any mystique that surrounds home curing – it is, at heart, a very simple procedure. Today we may think of these processes as being specialized and professional. But in times past everyone who raised livestock of any kind had a basic knowledge of how to use salt and smoke to help spread the goodness throughout the year. And everyone, whether small farmer or keen city cook, still can.

Of course, some of the items that Steven explores with such relish require more application than others. They are as much projects as recipes and may take half a day to put together and a long time to mature – weeks, sometimes months. For some you will need to invest in special equipment (a robust mincer, for example, and a sausage stuffer) or large quantities of ingredients (such as big cuts of meat or whole sacks of salt).

But the rewards for your dedication, for any extra outlay or time, are immense. Curing meat or smoking fish doesn't only result in a delicious end product; the gift is much greater than that. These are processes that unlock the secrets of some of our best-loved, most useful ingredients. They give you the keys to the citadel of smoky, salty-sweet-savory tastiness: the hallowed place where bacon, air-dried ham, smoked salmon, and kippers dwell. That may sound a bit over the top, but I stand by it. Because, let's be honest, preserving and flavoring your own food in this way is pretty cool. If, like me, you love not just the finished dish but the process itself, then making a bacon sandwich with pork belly that you've cured yourself or whittling some wafer-thin slices from a leg of your very own air-dried ham represents a kind of culinary nirvana. It doesn't get much better.

These techniques are empowering. As Steven points out, once you've salted a whole piece of pork and successfully air-dried it in your own backyard, you'll feel no curing challenge is out of reach. You'll realize that you have the capacity to produce wholly authentic, traditional charcuterie – you are an artisan! And every time you follow one of the recipes in this book, your confidence will grow.

You're in very good hands here. Steven Lamb is an absolute linchpin of the whole River Cottage operation and has been for a decade. He and I go back to the early days, when River Cottage HQ was a scrubbed-out cow barn with a secondhand kitchen rammed into a shed next door. He's shared our learning curve from the beginning, assisting with our earliest efforts in curing and smoking and building his knowledge through experiment and experience. He is now our go-to guy for all things salty and smoky.

Steven's knowledge is as broad as it is deep. He currently guides River Cottage visitors through everything from building clay bread ovens to butchering pigs. But it's as the teacher on our meat curing and smoking courses that he has achieved guru status, with both his River Cottage colleagues and the many hundreds he has taught over the years. That's no surprise: quite apart from the fact that his *coppa* is, hands-down, the best I've ever tasted, Steven is relentlessly passionate about this subject. He has a never-ending fascination for charcuterie and *salumi*, for cures and brines, for the subtle interplay of salt, smoke, and time. It's been a joy to see him pass this passion on to the people he teaches, and I'm thrilled he is now doing the same for readers of this brilliant book.

So, set aside any thoughts you may have about successful curing being beyond you. If you have some salt, pepper, and sugar in your cupboard (or frankly, even just some salt!), you're ready to go. You can start experimenting now with a good strip of pork or plump piece of fish. Next time, perhaps you'll add your own blend of herbs and spices to the cure, or you'll press an old cookie tin into service as a hot smoker to enhance that cured flesh even further. With this twanging new string to your culinary bow, you're well on your way to being a more versatile, accomplished, and ultimately fulfilled cook.

Hugh Fearnley-Whittingstall, East Devon, January 2014

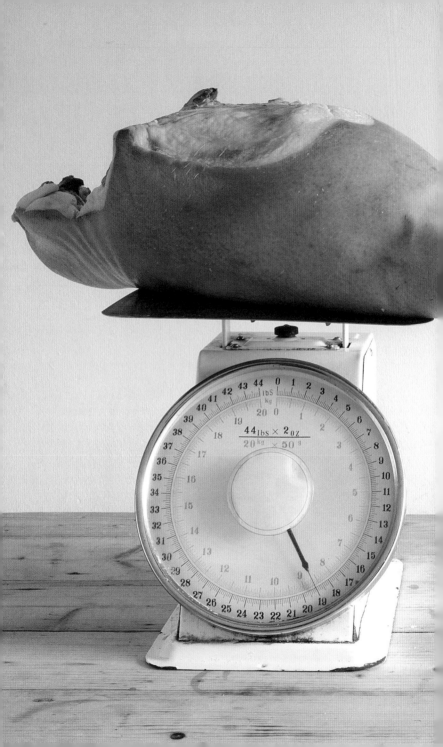

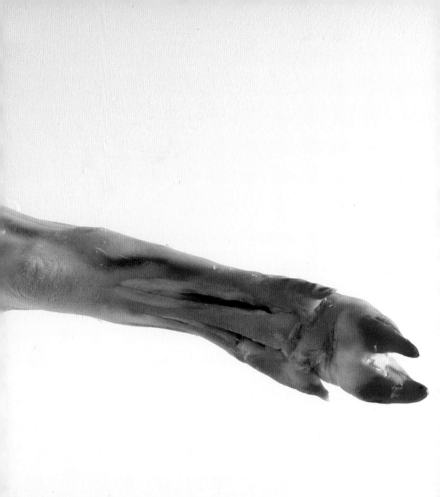

Tradition & Science

Real delicatessens are magical places. By "real,"

I mean stocked with authentic, artisan-made products and independently run. For me, these places are the equivalent of the candy store to a young child or the church to a believer. I could spend an age looking at hams, sausages, and salami, sizing up the interplay of ingredients, craftsmanship, culture, and geography that goes to make each unique item. It is not unusual to find me staring wide-eyed in wonderment at an array of charcuterie, muttering under my breath about the possible methods used to get to the final results and mentally working backward to their original source. I have the incurable River Cottage affliction of wanting to know the whole story of an ingredient, all the ins and outs of it, and I will pepper with questions whoever is on the other side of the counter in my bid to unlock the secrets. It is fair to say that I have an unholy reverence for cured products.

My obsession actually stems from a rather unexpected place. As a young boy in the 1970s, my mother would stockpile cans of Pek chopped pork and find umpteen ways of serving it to my brother and me – especially, as I recall, when we were on holiday. Dozens of cans, placed in a box, would be the first thing packed into the car. My mother is a fantastic cook, but despite her best intentions – and with a tight budget to feed us on – the experience was never less than awful. Whether it was given pride of place in a bread roll, scattered in a salad, or fried and served with a pineapple hat, the stuff was always bland, tasteless, and alien. We used to call it "pet-shop pork." She had an inverted snobbery as far as it was concerned: it was never to be referred to as Spam because that was too common, a name that belittled the exotic nature of this versatile lump of pork in a can from Poland.

Any interest I had in charcuterie might have been quashed by this early exposure to the bland, pretend end of it. Instead, I took the view that anything else would surely be an improvement. And so at every opportunity I would try any food that had its origins in the tradition of curing. I sampled corned beef and hams – cured in honey or molasses, brined, roasted, and sliced wafer-thin. I tasted salami rolled in black pepper, with chile seeds that made me catch my breath, and cold smoked salmon run through scrambled eggs on Christmas morning.

Everything was worth exploring and almost everything I tried I liked (with the exception of tripe with vinegar and onions). What began as an attempt to redress the balance for all the Pek chopped pork I had endured became an adventure, a journey. I felt myself becoming a little more sophisticated with each new taste, as if I were absorbing some of the culture and tradition behind the product as well as the flavors.

When holidays became slightly more elaborate and involved traveling abroad, I could hardly believe my luck. While everyone else was pulling faces at the sight of a Continental breakfast, I would be delighted at being given the chance to eat ham, pastrami, salami, and smoked cheese first thing in the morning. The obsession

Mortadella

Air-dried prosciutto

grew – I wanted to experience the most authentic versions of cured foods. For a while, only products in stalls in market squares in Spain, Italy, and France, sold by the people who actually made it, would satisfy me.

The pinnacle of my tasting journey (so far) was not one of the big players, such as Ibérico or serrano ham, but a morsel of *soppressata* eaten in Tuscany, cut from a hanging salami barely a week old, spread on a slice of warm bruschetta by the owner of a small bar up in the hills. That might seem a bit cavalier to those of you with a keen sense of basic food hygiene, but I was caught up in the moment. And it was wonderful, a taste that seemed to encapsulate all the romance and tradition of curing and smoking.

However, I live in deepest Dorset, not in central Europe, and although there are now some very good producers of both artisanal and commercial cured products in this country, it was only a matter of time before I started to experiment with producing my own cured delicacies. And the results astounded me. I've been curing and smoking my own meats, fish, and cheese for several years now, and I have a passion for guiding other people who want to do the same.

Our European cousins have never lost the connection between food and culture, and they have allowed their curing and smoking traditions to thrive – a fact that makes me extremely happy but ever so slightly envious. Yet there's no reason why we shouldn't be enjoying our own fantastic smoked and cured products here. We had the tradition in Britain but somehow forgot about it. Instead of passing on the expertise and recipes that our great-grandparents or great-great-grandparents would have known, we just stopped using them. But that disassociation is only in our heads. And I am glad to say that there are already some very fine new purveyors of this traditional craft breaking through, exploring afresh the methods that were part of our past. With this book, I'd like to be part of that resurgence.

It fills me with pleasure that both of my lovely young daughters have inherited the charcuterie gene. A recent trip to Spain saw them scoffing chorizo and chomping on *morcilla* as if they were born to it. Why shouldn't we all? The age-old techniques of curing and smoking encompass craft, tradition, science, and sorcery, but in looking toward the Continent for inspiration, I am constantly reminded how accessible and uncomplicated curing and smoking can be.

The straightforward, traditional methods laid out here will enable anyone to produce fantastic, authentic results. Creating simple cured products will expand your knowledge of food and increase your repertoire of dishes from all over the globe. It will enable you to take good British ingredients and turn them into elevated versions of themselves, applying minimum intervention. If you're curious, then I hope this book will be the beginning of your own wonderful journey of experimentation and reward.

A history of curing and smoking

Curing and smoking are deeply rooted in food history. They are among the earliest fundamental cooking techniques and can be traced back to ancient civilizations such as the Egyptian. Initially, they were the result of a need to make use of whatever food was available and extend its life so that communities could be sustained throughout the barren months. The process of curing food (through the application of salt), or of smoking it, has a dehydrating effect. In the days before refrigeration, this drying-out process was crucial for preserving food because it is moisture that fosters bacterial growth and leads to spoilage. Fortuitously, both salting and smoking have positive effects on flavor, too.

Examples of traditional cured and smoked foods can be found throughout the world, in both sophisticated and apparently primitive societies. For example, the Japanese produce a seasoning called *katsuobushi*: tuna fillets air-dried, smoked intermittently over a month, and then left to ferment in the sun until they resemble wooden blocks covered in mold. Fine shavings are planed off and added to dishes as a topping, in a similar way to Parmesan. Meanwhile, the Inuit people of northern Greenland have a centuries-old method of preserving meat that produces something called *kiviaq*. Small Arctic birds called auks are stuffed into the fatty skin of a slaughtered seal, which is then sewn up, buried under rocks in the cold ground, and left to ferment over a period of months before being eaten raw.

There is the intriguing question of how these methods came about in the first place. What made the first Inuit or Japanese person come to the conclusion that these processes would yield good results? It is impossible to know for sure, but their significance is clear. Both of these examples were – and still are – efficient ways of preserving food over the harsh winter months, an effective response to the basic need to survive.

Trying conditions and a paucity of ingredients have never stood in the way of progress in the arts of curing and smoking. In fact, hardship and difficulty have been their very lifeblood, forcing invention and ingenuity. The processes have never been entirely fixed or locked down, but rather they have evolved, with success coming as a result of a true understanding of what is available and the best way to use it.

In this way, the landscape, the seasons, local breeds, the diet available to the livestock, and the weather itself have shaped different cured products from all over the world and fixed them in their own particular places. Ibérico ham, for instance, which is one of the finest air-dried hams in the world, is made only from the *pata negra* (black foot) pig in a specific part of Spain. And the best Ibérico comes from pigs fed on a diet of acorns from local oak-wood pastures. There is nothing else like it, which is part of its enduring appeal.

Cold smoked cheese and *merguez* sausages

Most of the recipes in this book illustrate the two main European styles of curing and smoking, charcuterie and *salumi*, although I have borrowed from eastern European methods as well. As their names suggest, the recipes largely originate from either France or Italy. They rely on slightly different techniques but follow the same fundamental principles. The differences between them are more to do with style and geographical origin than basic technique.

The word *charcuterie* is derived from the French *chair*, meaning "flesh," and *cuit*, meaning "cooked." Originally, *charcuterie* was used solely as a term to describe preserved pork products, but it now encompasses products made from a wider selection of meats. Traditional charcuterie items include confit, sausages, pâtés, terrines, and hams.

Salumi is the Italian word used to describe any cured or smoked meat, such as salami, prosciutto, *coppa*, *guanciale*, or *bresaola*.

There are also recipes here for bacon, ham, and smoked fish – great cured products that stem from our own British curing tradition. Homemade bacon, as it happens, is one of the very best recipes with which to begin your own curing adventure (see pp. 138–43).

Both the Continental and British styles of curing draw on very old, traditional culinary methods, and there are various rules that should be adhered to – more on that later. But what excites me about them is that, within the confines of each method, there is room for you to exercise a little individuality and introduce the ingredients that suit your palate. Curing and smoking continue to evolve with every generation, and the minute you decide to make your first bit of home-cured bacon, you become part of the story. As well as drawing from the tradition, your own experience adds to it.

Traditional cured foods

As with most artisan-made things, there is a threat to the existence of traditional cured foods. Although most of these crafts are still practiced in the original way at least somewhere, the majority of them are also replicated using more commercial methods. For every authentic cured product, there is an antithesis: a factory-made, mass-produced alternative that usually bears the same name but few or none of the original qualities.

The fast-food, accelerated version of smoking and curing culture is perhaps now the most prominent. By which I mean if you go and buy any of the classic cured products, such as air-dried ham, salami, or bacon, the chances are you will get a mass-produced version. This is even true in Italy and France, the homes of *salumi* and charcuterie.

This is, of course, the way of the world, but it makes me uneasy. Even the most well-intentioned large-scale manufacturers who want to make something very good have to think about their bottom line. Generally, mass production eradicates the hard-won collective knowledge that led to a product's original identity. It kills off the craft because factories need to churn out large volumes – quickly and cheaply. There is no room for the practice of patience.

However, the news is not all bad – far from it. In many parts of Europe, while the commercial machine has trundled on inexorably, it hasn't steamrollered all the traditional producers in the process. In Britain, more and more traditional producers are appearing, although they still account for just 1 percent of the charcuterie and *salumi* consumed here. The original crafts have remained and, in some places, flourished. In fact, these are good times for lovers of cured foods, as long as you are discerning.

More and more cured products are protected by laws that uphold their quality and authenticity. PDO status (Protected Designation of Origin), attached to products such as prosciutto, *culatello*, and *lardo*, is becoming more widespread. The recently launched New Nordic food movement, for instance, has captured the collective imagination, as well as political support, in and around Scandinavia. It manages to promote local, traditional foods while delivering at a modern, commercial level by helping small producers supply top-end restaurants such as Noma in Copenhagen. Similarly, in Italy, the Slow Food movement has protected traditional products from an influx of foreign fast-food alternatives and now has charitable status.

It won't come as any surprise to read that I am a champion of the traditional, old-fashioned approach. I want it to be a continuation and reflection of the skilled craftsmanship that inspired me in the first place and, for that reason, I have the home-curing enthusiast, rather than the commercial operator, in mind here.

I do not, however, mean to denigrate anyone who wants to try curing or smoking on a commercial scale. Nor do I think being commercially successful is synonymous with the abandonment of tradition. There are some very fine producers who manage to balance the commercial and the artisanal. A variety of important issues must be considered, however. Anyone who prepares cured foods needs to think about the nature of his or her ingredients, but the commercial processor must also adhere to the regulations and recommendations of the local and national agencies that oversee standards that relate to the selling of food (see pp. 36–39).

The Principles

In order to start curing and smoking, it is important to understand the basic science behind the techniques and how the main ingredients interact to flavor and preserve.

Fresh meat does not have a very long shelf life. Once it stops being part of a living animal, it begins to deteriorate under the influence of enzymes, oxygen, and light. This process is not entirely negative: it can improve texture as well as flavor, as in the example of aged beef. However, ultimately, meat that is left unadulterated will spoil.

Bacteria thrive on the surface of meat and will multiply infinitely if you let them, while the moisture and fats break down over time and turn the meat rancid. (Meats that carry a higher percentage of saturated fat, such as beef or pork, take longer to spoil than those with more unsaturated fat, such as poultry or fish.) In curing and smoking, we are applying ingredients and creating conditions that either arrest deterioration or control the process so that it can happen safely over an extended period.

The key to curing meat successfully is the reduction or eradication of moisture. This creates an environment that is not only inhospitable to the bacteria that cause products to spoil but also, crucially, beneficial for microbes that protect the meat and add flavor. For, as well as preventing the growth of the unwelcome bacteria that cause spoilage, we actually want to attract specific bacteria, namely halophiles (meaning "salt lovers").

These beneficial bacteria thrive in dry, salty conditions. When in contact with meat, they create lactic acid, which both protects the meat from pathogenic bacteria such as listeria and encourages desirable molds such as penicillium, which will also work to your advantage. If salt is used in the right way, the food will become stable. Over time, it will continue to dry out, and eventually, it will get too hard to eat, but it will never go bad.

Smoking complements salting. Smoke, of course, adds a spectrum of complex flavors that can enhance a huge range of ingredients, but it also has a preservative effect. Phenol, a compound within smoke, acts as an antioxidant that inhibits the rancidification of fat, while naturally occurring formaldehyde and acetic acid lower the pH (increase the acidity) when deposited on the surface of meat, fish, or poultry, which has an antimicrobial effect.

Salted meat

Salt and fat

Curing is a layer of love applied to something that you already hold a deep affection for. And it is the crucial ingredients – salt and fat – that really fuel the affair. Of course, there are health issues related to these key players. However, those issues are connected to consuming them in excess. Granted, if you ate nothing but bacon, chorizo, and ham, you would have cause for concern, but modest quantities of home-cured produce, consumed as part of a balanced diet, can be enjoyed without anxiety.

When you read through some of my recipes, you may be surprised at some of the quantities of salt and fat listed. But please remember those are the quantities needed to successfully preserve that particular ingredient, which may be a very large piece of meat. When you sit down to eat a portion of it, you will be consuming only a tiny fraction of the original salt and fat.

Salt

In all curing and preserving methods there is one common denominator: sodium chloride. This is just ordinary, everyday salt. However, used in the right way, it is a truly miraculous substance. If all of the ingredients known to man were lined up against a wall in preparation for the biggest imaginable cook-off of all time, I would pick out salt first and make it my team captain.

Sodium chloride is, quite literally, the salt of the earth, a primeval mineral, released by the natural erosion of rocks in the world's oceans or mined from deep underground. Much attention is given to the dangers of consuming too much salt and of course we should all be mindful of our intake. But salt is most harmful when it is hidden – as it is in many commercially processed foods – so that you can be consuming excessive amounts without realizing it.

It is easy to forget that salt is nevertheless essential – a nutrient our bodies cannot do without. Nerve and muscle cells (including those in the heart) generate electrical energy by creating an imbalance of sodium across a cell membrane. If a body is deficient in sodium, it struggles to do this, leading to muscle weakness and neurological problems.

Salt is also unbelievably useful when used wisely: it has been employed for thousands of years, across every geographical region on earth, to enhance food and extend its natural life. Salt has traveled through time with us, seasoning and preserving what we eat.

Salt can be applied to food to suppress flavors as well as enhance them. It elevates natural tastes and aromas but also softens bitterness. It is a mineral that has been the basis of survival for many of the ancient civilizations we deem to be advanced, such as the Egyptian and Roman. It has even been used as a currency, particularly on trading routes in the ancient world. It was also known as "white gold." A Roman soldier's pay was called *salarium*, from the Latin *sal* for "salt," because the soldiers used it to buy salt; our word *salary* comes from this. Salt remains central in just about every kitchen across the planet.

The preservative ability of salt stems from its unique molecular structure. It is comprised of small, highly concentrated, superbusy, positively and negatively charged atoms that penetrate other foods. Salt draws out moisture, which limits the growth of the microbes that cause meat to spoil. The salt itself then travels in the opposite direction, into the meat, and promotes the benign bacteria that bring flavor. This subtle, gradual exchange is known as osmosis, and it happens to be one of my favorite transactions related to food.

By drastically slowing down deterioration, salt creates a window of opportunity for flavor to develop. Within the meat, enzymes digest natural sugars and then release lactic or acetic acid (an enzyme is, in essence, a substance produced by a living organism that acts as a catalyst to bring about a biochemical reaction). These acids in turn break down proteins and fats into smaller molecules, such as peptides. Over the course of several weeks or months, peptides convert into a complex array of flavorsome compounds with citrus and nutty notes.

As well as drawing out moisture and drying the meat, therefore starving and killing off unwanted microorganisms (and imparting flavor), salt also alters its texture and appearance. A concentration of salt loosens the protein strands in the muscle cells, which are usually grouped together tightly, causing them to separate. This weakens the fibers, which gives cured meats a silky tenderness and slightly translucent appearance.

You'll find information about the specific types of salt I recommend for use in curing and smoking on pp. 82–83.

Fat

Although often talked about as a single, malign entity, there are many different kinds of fat, some of which are known to be beneficial when consumed in the right quantities. There are fats, or rather elements of fat, such as omega-3 and omega-6 fatty acids, that are considered essential but on the whole, should you choose to, you could probably survive without consuming fat in your diet. It would, however, be a miserable culinary experience, and I, for one, would never choose to do that. Fat is where flavor resides, and it is a fantastic commodity in both domestic and commercial kitchens.

Fat was an everyday ingredient when I was growing up. Beef drippings had pride of place in the pantry, and my dad would spread them on everything, like a master plasterer at work. In our house, pork crackling could start a fight. My mum kept a frying pan of fat constantly on the go: it was used for every breakfast, placed

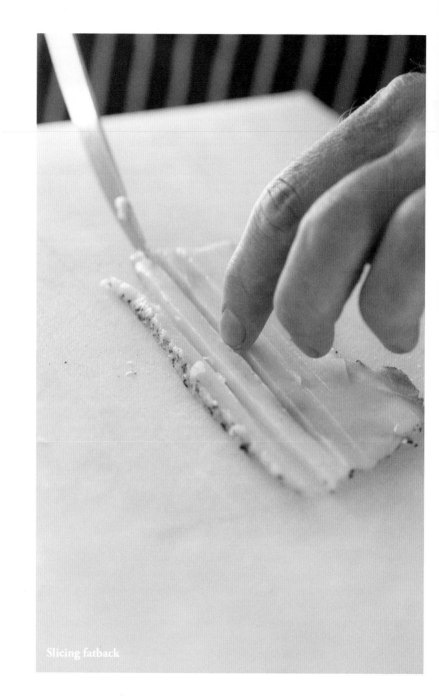
Slicing fatback

on the stove top until the solid fat had rendered and started to spit. At that point, bacon would be placed into the hot fat, followed by eggs and bread. Once the cooking had been completed, the fat, still in the pan, would be put to the back of the stove and allowed to cool and set again, ready for the next time. It was a magic pan that never lost any of its contents and woke from its solid, creamy white slumber to become clear and liquid over and over again. I loved that battered, blue-handled, fat-filled pan and expect it to be bequeathed to me when my mum is ready to hand it on, our one family heirloom.

I realize that some of you reading this are likely to be appalled! We have been encouraged to cut down on fat, and animal fats in particular – the very fats, as it happens, that are most useful in the curing process. We are constantly informed that eating fat causes high cholesterol, which will ultimately lead to heart disease. But it is a common misconception that all animal fats are saturated and that all are bad for you.

Our consumption of animal fats cannot be blamed entirely for the alarming increase in obesity levels, high cholesterol, and related health problems. Over the last sixty years or so, the population as a whole has become much less active and the quality of our diets has deteriorated, with too much reliance on overly processed food, especially cheap high-energy sugary foods and drinks.

Traditional fats such as lard and butter have been demonized, and "healthier" alternatives, such as margarine and vegetable oils, have flooded the shelves. But these are not necessarily healthier options. Margarine, in particular, is a source of harmful trans fats. Perhaps it is time we took a more balanced view on animal fats. It is, after all, a case of moderation.

Avoiding animal fats not only robs us of flavor, but has also meant that animal husbandry and breeding practices have changed for the worse. As consumers, we have become suspicious of visible fat left on meat; we assume it's there to add weight and cost. Animals are therefore bred to be leaner these days. The introduction of large white pigs in this country almost killed off the traditional, slow-growing breeds that put flavorsome layers of fat on top of wonderful meat. They are now called rare breeds for a reason.

In addition, when flavor is seen as less important than leanness, the conditions in which animals are kept generally deteriorate. Living in cramped quarters without access to natural light and unable to indulge in all their natural behaviors, they are not allowed to mature properly, and this is reflected in the lack of fat and flavor in the meat that they produce.

The use of fat – pork fat in particular – is crucial in the curing process, not least because it keeps the flavor and texture in your meat while it loses moisture. On p. 81, you will find more about the specific types of fat that are used. I, for one, will continue to enjoy fat, in sensible quantities, without qualms.

Bacteria

The processes of curing and smoking can be understood on one level as the introduction and rebuffing of bacteria and molds. These may not be particularly appetizing terms, which is why the marketing industry uses words like *aging* and *maturing* to describe the effects of these microorganisms. It is more appealing to talk about "well-hung beef," for instance, than "decomposing flesh." Similarly, molds may be described as "benign blooms" that dust the surface of meat or cheese, though it would be equally accurate to describe them as "incubating" and "multiplying" microorganisms.

At the end of the day, it all boils down to the same thing: a controlled aging process. And, whichever way you choose to phrase it, when it comes to home curing, you are the agent of that control, the first and last line of defense – the head of security at the microbe club.

Bacteria, like it or not, are already playing an active, if invisible, role in your daily life. They are present in every environment, and our bodies house hundreds of different types. There are probably at least one hundred different bacteria on this page alone and many more on the skin of your hand. Bacteria are particularly prominent in food, and especially in cured, uncooked meat, so you can see why you need to develop a fine understanding of their positive and negative qualities.

In fact, very few bacteria are working against us. On the whole, they perform an important role in keeping us functioning, helping us digest and metabolize food. Any bad bacteria are generally dealt with by our immune system, but there are some that you simply don't want to meet.

Rather like basic, minute single-cell versions of humans, bacteria consume food, create waste, and reproduce. Bacteria are most active in a warm environment (between 79°F and 95°F) and like a wet situation, so they are partial, for instance, to water or blood.

Raw meat is high in water – up to 80 percent – and therefore a favorable place for bacteria, which, in the right conditions, will multiply quickly. The level of liquid present in raw meat is crucial in the curing process: too much liquid promotes bad bacterial growth and makes the meat "turn," or spoil. The application of salt – and also, to some extent, cold smoke – is a key way in which we reduce the water content in meat and thereby preserve it. When salt is applied to meat it creates a high concentration of dissolved sodium and chloride ions within the meat. The water inside the muscle cells is drawn out because of the effect of osmolarity, or pressure, and the salt is absorbed.

Additionally, in very high-salt solutions, such as wet-cure brines, many microbes will rupture, owing to the difference in pressure between the outside and inside of the organism. Most bacteria, with the exception of the beneficial halophiles ("salt-loving" bacteria), cannot grow in conditions where the level of salt is greater than 3 percent. Solutions with a high concentration of sugar have the same effect on microbes, which is why sugar is used as a preservative in jams and jellies and also in a basic dry cure or brine.

Salt also increases acidity, lowering the pH in the meat and making it less hospitable to microbes that cause spoilage. The perfect pH in cured meat is 4.5 to 5, which inhibits unwanted bacterial growth but allows benign white powdery molds and airborne yeasts to spore on the surface. These contribute additional flavors by denaturing the bacterial acids on the surface, giving dry-cured, air-dried meat that tangy, aromatic flavor.

The wrong types of bacteria not only create sour or off flavors, but can also cause illness and, in the very worst-case scenario, death. So there is no place for a cavalier attitude with curing. The chances of contracting an illness from food-borne bacteria are minimal, but that is no reason to stick your head in the sand. General good hygiene and correctly applied curing techniques should eliminate unwanted bacterial activity. But some curing methods, such as fermentation in the making of salami, are carried out within a potentially hazardous temperature range and the finished product is then eaten uncooked, which adds to the risk, so additional care must be taken. These are the areas of curing where the potential use of artificial antibacterial substances – namely nitrates, nitrites, and starter cultures – comes to the fore.

Bacteria are not visible to the eye and therefore you cannot see if any negative bacteria are present. Of course, if a salami or cured ham leg was dripping black liquid and smelling awful, you could determine that it wasn't in the best shape to eat. However, bad bacteria don't always present themselves in such an obvious way. That is why it is important to be precise with measurements and careful about curing conditions: these are your only ways of controling the cure (if you decide not to add nitrates and starter cultures).

Molds

Just as there are good and bad bacteria, there are desirable and undesirable molds. However, molds are a slightly less scary subject because they are mostly benign (there is little or no risk that the wrong mold will kill you), and they are visible to the naked eye. Also, molds grow at a much slower rate than bacteria (which, in the right conditions, can multiply into the millions from a standing start in under ten hours).

With molds, there is a greater element of control. They are only ever present on the surface of foods because they are aerobic (require oxygen), and so they cannot

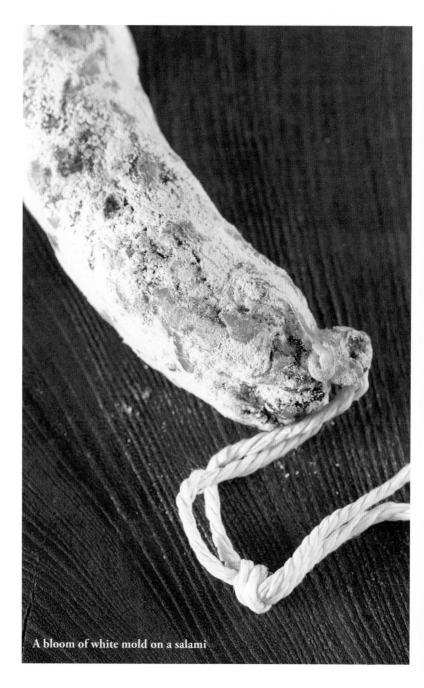

A bloom of white mold on a salami

hide unnoticed in the middle of a salami. In extreme cases, you can get molds that release poisonous mycotoxins, but these tend to affect only grains or vegetables.

In most curing, the desired mold is a very distinct chalky-white variety known as penicillium. This is similar to the blue mold you find in some cheeses (which is deliberately placed there by the cheese maker). Not only does it contribute to the overall flavor of the cured product but it also performs three very important functions. Firstly, once the mold is present on the surface, it will grow to cover the entire surface, thereby inhibiting any harmful bacteria from getting a foothold. Secondly, it consumes oxygen and thereby reduces the process of oxidation in the cured product itself. Oxidation discolors and causes off flavors. Lastly, it forms a barrier between the surface of the cured product and the natural light that can turn fat rancid.

Quite often, you'll come across other molds on your cured foods – green, orange, or black – and sometimes in fuzzy, long fronds. These undesirable molds are due mostly to an absence of air movement around the curing meat or too much warmth. Stagnant air generally causes the wrong molds because the humidity levels are too high. Perfect air-drying humidity levels are between 60 and 80 percent, where the benevolent penicillia prosper.

However, these unwelcome molds do not indicate that the meat is off (not unless it is actually black and dripping, with a rancid smell!). You can clean off unwanted molds with a cloth or nailbrush dampened in malt vinegar. This has antimicrobial qualities and will also increase the acidity on the surface of the food, which tends to promote the penicillium mold that you want.

If you don't find the right mold growing on your cured meats, you can put it there yourself. You can buy a commercial culture, dissolve it in distilled water, then apply the solution to the meat, or simply dip the meat into it. These cultures are available online from butcher supplies websites.

Alternatively, you can hang inexpensive store-bought salami next to one of your own curing salami, and the mold will simply travel from the finished product to your own. What's more, the beneficial microflora will then always be present in the area that you have designated as your air-drying spot for curing, which is a very good thing.

I have seen molds of all types on cured food, both homemade and commercial products. My inbox is full of pictures of moldy meat from all over the world! The rule of thumb should be to use the vinegar technique to clean off any mold that doesn't look powdery and white, check temperatures and humidity levels regularly, and wait for the mold to come back in the desirable form. This will not harm the curing process. It just means that the flavor won't be as mature until the mold is present.

Nitrates and nitrites

You will have heard, I am sure, of a potentially fatal disease called botulism. This very nasty illness is caused by toxins released by *Clostridium botulinum* bacteria. Botulism is rare, but of course, it has to be taken very seriously. The *C. botulinum* bacterium is found in soil and in aquatic sediments all over the globe. It remains dormant and unthreatening unless its environment becomes warm, moist, low in acidity, and oxygen-free. The bacteria themselves are not harmful, but the toxins they produce are highly poisonous. The bacteria can be killed by cooking at a high temperature for a significant time. Most cases of food-borne botulism are caused by food being kept at the wrong temperature or being badly stored, or through bad practice at commercial canning factories.

Although good hygiene and correct technique should ensure that botulism is never able to take a hold, there is one way to be absolutely sure, and that is by using nitrates and nitrites in curing. It is the belt-and-braces way of eradicating this baddie and is viewed as a necessity in most commercial meat-curing operations. However, some artisanal producers choose not to utilize these chemical compounds because they are not natural additives.

The use of nitrates and nitrites is a subject that often splits opinion, not just among producers, but also among scientists and physicians. I would like to help you navigate through this tricky subject. I don't use synthetic cures myself, but I want you to make up your own mind.

The nitrates and nitrites commonly used in commercially cured meat products are found in preprepared mixes of curing salts, which may be called instacure, Prague powders, or pink salt. (Most cure mixes are colored pink to prevent accidental ingestion; however, the pink color of Himalayan salt is naturally occurring.) These synthetic cures (sodium nitrate and sodium nitrite) are produced by chemical reaction. The salt is prepared in a lab by treating sodium hydroxide with mixtures of nitrogen dioxide and nitric oxide:

$$2\ NaOH + NO_2 + NO \rightarrow 2\ NaNO_2 + H_2O$$

Commercial curing salts are mostly divided into two categories, often referred to as cure #1 and cure #2.

Cure #1 This is a mixture of sodium nitrite (6.25 percent) and sodium chloride (93.75 percent). It is primarily used for curing whole-muscle products that are to be cold smoked, such as bacon. It is inadvisable to use nitrite-only cures, such as cure #1, in recipes that require a lengthy curing time because the nitrite gets used up (metabolized) relatively quickly.

Cure #2   This is a mixture of sodium nitrite (6.25 percent), sodium nitrate (4 percent), and sodium chloride (89.75 percent). It provides fast-acting protection against botulism from the nitrite, and a slower-release protection from the sodium nitrate. Cure #2 is used in salami that are to be cured over a long time. It should never be used on any product that will be fried at high temperatures, such as bacon, because of the resulting formation of nitrosamines (see overleaf).

Another product, Tender Quick, is comprised of 0.5 percent sodium nitrite and 0.5 percent sodium nitrate, plus sodium chloride, sugar, and propylene glycol (to keep the mix uniform). It is used primarily in the making of commercial brines.

Nitrates slowly react with naturally occurring bacteria and are converted into nitrites. Nitrites are then converted to nitric oxide. This raises the acidity levels that help prevent meat from spoiling. However, acidity levels are raised effectively just by adding salt, which also produces lactic acid, adding a tangy piquancy that nitrate-treated products lack.

Nitric oxide combines with myoglobin – the pigment that makes meat red – to form nitrosomyoglobin, which fixes a deep red color in uncooked dry sausage. Without nitrites, cured meat doesn't always retain the original color. For example, it is virtually impossible to replicate the pinkness of a commercial slice of corned beef without using the color-fixing properties of nitrites.

Nitrites also act on the fibers of whole muscles of meat, giving them firmness and a slight sheen. This effect used to fuel my concerns about using nitrites because I thought they might possibly have the same effect on my physiology. (I could do with it in some areas, but you don't have that control!) In fact, most of the nitrites are excreted from the body well before they have any effect on muscle tissue.

Adding nitrates as part of the curing process is not a new thing. Potassium nitrate (saltpeter) was used as early as the fifteenth century, and although it is viewed a little negatively these days (because of its other use, in explosives), it is still available and used throughout Europe. However, most producers use lab-prepared sodium nitrate.

It is possible to create safe, authentic cured products without the use of nitrates and nitrites. We've been doing it at River Cottage for a long time, and this tradition is widespread throughout Europe. In order to ensure safety of the finished product, the most important factors are to get the temperature, humidity, and acidity correct at all times (particularly during the fermentation process of making salami). Using good-quality raw materials and applying strict hygiene controls are also crucial.

Although nitrates and nitrites are added to many commercially cured foods, it is only really necessary for them to be added to meat that has been minced for making salami, in order to stop pathogenic bacteria growing. Botulism bacteria cannot grow on the exterior surface of meat but could thrive within the airless interior of salami, which is cured and dried at, or around, normal room temperature. One of the main beneficial qualities of nitrates and nitrites is that they function within the same temperature range at which bad bacteria thrive (79°F to 95°F), and over a long period, so their use allows products such as salami to be cured for 6 to 8 weeks, unrefrigerated, free from any risk of botulism.

You can, however, cure salami at home without added nitrates or nitrites by applying the correct amount of salt. The minimum amount of salt required is 2 percent. If you then follow the procedures on p. 103 and hang salami in the perfect drying conditions, you will have no need for synthetic cure powders.

If you want to make salami-style products and you're in any doubt about your own environment or processes, I suggest you use synthetic cures containing nitrates and nitrites. The minimum level of synthetic cure mix is 0.08 ounce for every 2.2 pounds of meat (in addition to conventional salt, of course).

So why don't I use these synthetic cures? Put simply, they are antithetical to my approach, which is to use the most natural ingredients and the most traditional methods that I can. Also, pure sodium nitrite is quite toxic to humans.

In addition, there are major concerns regarding the carcinogenic properties of nitrates, particularly when they are exposed to high temperatures – as when bacon is cooked. This can create compounds called nitrosamines, which can potentially cause cancer. Opinion is split on the precise levels required for such a devastating effect, although it is unlikely that the amount of nitrates used in commercially cured and processed meat is unsafe to this degree.

There is another dilemma here for anyone wanting to follow the authentic, natural route. Although all of the above nitrite and nitrate mixes categorically stop pathogenic bacteria from forming and therefore remove the risk of botulism, they also introduce an element of the nonorganic to your product. There are some synthetic cures on the market that are advertized as organic, but none comes from the government with a stamp of approval.

I have to concede, though, that nitrates and nitrites do also occur naturally. You find them in green vegetables such as spinach and celery. In fact, our metabolism frequently converts nitrates into nitrites as part of digestion: while the majority of them are excreted in our urine, some remain in the acidic environment of our stomachs, aiding digestion.

There are other, natural alternatives to commercial cure mixes, such as celery salt. The celery plant needs a soil high in nitrogen to thrive, and its seeds are rich in nitrates. These can be substituted for synthetic sodium nitrate in meat curing and have the same effect on salami as a synthetic nitrate. Celery extracts have very little pigment and a mild taste that does not detract from the flavor of the meat. They may be listed as natural flavorings on product labels. In addition, celery salt also contains high levels of antioxidants, which help your body process the nitrates.

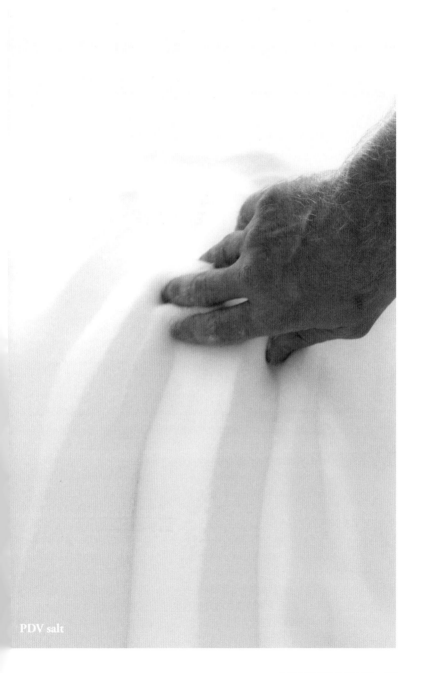

PDV salt

Ham hock and brine bin

The downside to using celery salt, and it is a considerable downside, is that there is absolutely no way of regulating, or even knowing, how much nitrate it contains. So, even if you use the same amount of celery salt in every salami cure you make, the amount of nitrate present could vary dramatically. Celery salt is not for me because its use involves sheer guesswork.

Salt naturally contains nitrates and nitrites as well as a myriad of other minerals. Even though they occur in lower amounts than in synthetic cures, the action of salt in the right amounts has the same, if not superior, effect.

The decision as to whether or not to use nitrates or nitrites is a difficult one, particularly if you want to create traditional, authentic salami and cold smoked products. There are certainly strong arguments for and against. Suffice it to say, though, that at River Cottage, we do not add any nitrites or nitrates to our cured food. We do not believe you need them as long as you follow best practice, add the right percentage of salt, and keep the curing products in the right conditions.

We follow traditional methods, ones that are governed and championed by the likes of the Slow Food movement, but have the advantage of modern scientific knowledge. We can apply precisely the correct ratio of salt and monitor pH levels (low acidity being a critical factor in the development of botulism), as well as air-drying in the best conditions so that humidity and temperature are perfect.

Bear in mind, also, that it is only really for fermented sausages, salami, and items that are to be cold smoked that the question of nitrates and nitrites comes up at all. You could stick to air-dried hams, unsmoked bacon, and *coppa* and avoid the issue altogether.

Every cure is different

No matter how much I learn about the science of curing, it has never lessened for me the romance and excitement of it. One of the things I love about this craft (and this can be seen as an advantage of not using synthetic cure mixes) is that you will always find subtle differences among all the cured products you create. This is what I think of as the sorcery of curing, by which I mean the magic worked on a product by the unique ingredients that go into it and the environment in which it is made.

So, for instance, although I always make salami in essentially the same way, I still know that when I slice into a new one, it will be slightly, subtly different from the last. I love this element of the unknown, which sets every product apart and is really the final celebration of the process. If you have followed the method, used the key ingredients in the correct ratios, and allowed the process to happen in the appropriate conditions, then this revelation of the unknown will always be a pleasant surprise and will engage the senses in new ways.

Commercial considerations

The main difference between domestic and commercial production of cured foods is the legal requirement to use nonnatural preservatives containing sodium nitrites and sodium nitrates. If you do not use these, then your home-cured products should be only for home consumption or consumption among friends, family, and "general extended parties." You are not permitted to sell them commercially.

One key step, should you want to embark on a commercial operation, is to get the government agencies involved with health and safety issues and licensing on your side and working with you from the outset. Too many people enter into the commercial production process with the idea already formed that these bodies are there to be prohibitive. This simply isn't true or helpful.

In some cases, the officers of these agencies may not fully understand what you are trying to do, particularly if you are hoping to stick closely to traditional, artisanal methods. But that just makes it doubly important for you to convey, at the earliest opportunity, the importance of traditional methods to your business – without, of course, sounding as if you have a total disregard for health and safety law. In short, get them to understand your business plan and your reasoning.

You will need to know about HACCPs (Hazard Analysis Critical Control Points). These are protocols for the production, storing, and selling of food – in effect, they are a set of operational guidelines that also act as a risk assessment system so that at any given point, from production to sale, there is an audit trail and accountability. These guidelines are written by you with the help of government officers, so that you can actively show them your high standards.

If you engage in the monitoring process willingly, and depending on individual local office compliance, you should be able to create a set of standards that are applicable to your own operation and may act as a pioneering template for other people's future businesses. Try to view this (admittedly not exciting) administrative task for what it is: vital work that enhances your operation because it shows good working practice.

Commercial food preparation standards

The correct handling of high-risk areas can mean the difference between a successful business run with the consent of the local governmental office overseeing food production standards and one that runs illegally that could potentially poison customer. All of the risk areas are controllable; they simply require common sense.

Personal hygiene Have a designated hand-wash area and always wash your hands with antibacterial soap.

Meat Never allow cooked, cured, and raw meats to come into contact with one another. Use separate areas and machinery for each item. Color coding of equipment such as knives and cutting boards is an industry standard practice.

Working area As well as complying with the obvious points about hygiene, your working area should be clearly defined and reflect what you look to produce.

Handling Any area that is used for processing or handling raw meat should have a cutting zone with all the equipment, such as meat grinders, sausage stuffers, slicers, and wrapping tables.

Chopping surfaces You should have a balance of both wooden cutting surfaces and stainless-steel work tops.

Cold storage and freezing These should be separate areas. It could be as simple as a fridge and a freezer, but it is unlikely that this would be sufficient for a business looking to process a number of different products. The cold storage would normally comprise an area or a walk-in unit that is chilled to 36°F, with a rail that large pieces of raw meat could be hung from, and a similar-size freezer unit with clearly labeled stacking shelves.

Dry curing areas If you want to have a designated dry curing area, consider a commercial unit, of which there are some on the market that tick all the right boxes. These professional models can be set for the appropriate temperature, humidity, and circulation of air with the capacity to cure salami or prosciutto at the touch of a button. They are also "reassuringly" expensive. If one of these units is a little out of your reach, you need to create another separate area where you can control and maintain the range of temperatures, humidity, and air movement that will suit the product as well as conform to the HACCP guidelines. This area should really operate at a temperature in the range of 50°F to 72°F, with a humidity level of 60 to 80 percent and with a system to circulate air. Buying a good thermo-hygrometer will enable you to measure humidity accurately (see p. 54).

Labeling You always need to be clear about labeling the product for sale. You must have your business head in place so that your products are priced competitively, as well as reflect the effort and length of time it takes to get them to point of sale.

Information on packaging Products that are packaged have to carry a labeling system showing the ingredients, net weight, use-by date, and price.

28·10·13 Salami £14·70 net weight 400g

Testing Finally, although it is not a legal requirement, it is good working practice to send, willingly and unprompted, one or two randomly chosen products to be lab tested for anything that might be considered harmful or dangerous. It is widely understood that cured meat products innately carry more than their fair share of bacteria and microorganisms, but, of course, the majority of them are encouraged or even introduced on purpose to benefit the process and final product. It is these positive bacteria that produce the unique taste and texture. However, the harmful bacteria that can occur through poor hygiene, incorrect handling, and lack of diligence and common sense could actually kill you. There is no place at all for health-and-safety roulette.

In accordance with the information given by government agencies, a good HACCP-based food-safety management system should

- be integral to the business, with all staff members knowledgeable about the requirements and what they have to do;
- be tailor-made to the needs of the business;
- include procedures for all food activities; and
- have procedures that are simple yet comprehensive.

Equipment

I have never been one for stockpiling shiny new equipment: it always seems to overpromise. Rather than empowering me, an abundance of appliances just makes me feel swamped and weighed down. This slight equipment phobia is something that I have had to address as I've explored the world of curing and smoking. But rest assured, I still rarely do anything by machine that can be done as well by hand, and I will not be trying to persuade you to spend an arm and a leg on gadgets and gizmos.

As a home-curing enthusiast, there may be some things you just cannot do without, but you need far less stuff and far less space than a commercial operator would, and your initial investment should be fairly minimal. Before spending any money, consider what you hope to produce and in what quantities, and always think about storage space. Aim to buy just the items of equipment you need to start off your home-curing venture.

As with most things, there is a close relationship between cost and quality when it comes to buying this sort of equipment. You shouldn't have to spend a small fortune, but the old adage of "buy cheap, buy twice" does usually apply. Occasionally, there are exceptions that prove this rule, such as the old Victorian hand-cranked grinder I picked up at a local garage sale for a couple of quid that has never let me down. It can be worth shopping around a little. But generally the best place to look for the essential bits of equipment is a butcher shop supply store or online. Often, you will find a "one-stop shop," set up to supply both the commercial sector and the home enthusiast, which should be able to meet all your needs.

Machinery

If you are going to be making your own cured goods on a regular basis, you will certainly need to invest in some machinery. You can always chop meat into coarse morsels with a sharp knife or cut relatively thin slices off a slab of bacon. You could, after a fashion, improvise with a funnel and rolling pin to make sausages. But with these tasks, you would most certainly never match the efficiency of a grinder, meat slicer, or sausage stuffer.

Meat grinder

In order to make successful salami, sausages, or pâtés, you will require a meat grinder. This allows you to grind fairly large quantities of meat, including variety meats, into even, appropriately sized grains or morsels easily. You need to cut the meat into pieces small enough to fit into the top hole of the feeding plate, from where it is moved along the chamber by a spiraled "worm." The meat is then cut by a rotating blade before being forced through the end plate and into a bowl.

Pork ground on the coarse plate

Adding salami mix to a sausage stuffer

Most grinders come with three detachable blades and plates that dictate the texture of the ground meat. Each plate has several holes in it of uniform diameter, usually ranging from ⅓ to ⅛ inch, to give the meat a coarse, medium, or fine texture. I favor the coarse plate for sausages and salami; the medium one for burgers or processing scraps, off cuts, and bits of "trim"; and the finer plate for pâtés.

It is important to always match the right blade with the right plate because the blades are self-sharpening. If they're used with the wrong plate, they will eventually become blunt. A blunt blade will "chew" meat and give it an unpleasant texture. Always tie the blade to the plate in a pair with butcher's string when it is not in use.

Apart from producing a lovely, clean-textured grind, the benefit of using a good meat grinder is that it will not transfer heat into its moving parts, so the temperature of the meat is not raised. To make sure none of the residual heat in the cleaned moving parts of the grinder transfers warmth to fresh meat during use, you should first cool the parts down in a deep tray of ice water, then dry and reassemble them ready for use.

You can grind meat in a food processor, but it may transfer some heat to the meat, and it will never give you the same evenly chopped texture as a proper grinder; the meat will be more of a coarse puree. I have had some success using a high-end domestic food processor, but I'd recommend you go for a good meat grinder. Superior models start at around $250; these are classed as domestic appliances. The model we use at River Cottage is designed for small- to medium-scale production and costs around $840.

Sausage stuffer

This allows you to force ground meat into a casing via a selection of nozzles. At the commercial end of the scale, there are automated sausage machines that fire out thousands of sausages in rapid succession from chambers that can hold hundreds of pounds of meat. However, all you need at home is a small, upright hand-cranked version with three nozzle attachments. You can pick up a reasonable one for around $170. As well as sausages, it can be used for salami, blood sausage, and a whole host of other recipes. This machine makes sausage filling painless and stress-free without being overly mechanical – you're still very much hands-on, since you slide on the sausage skins and load in the meat.

By and large, the individual components of sausage stuffers are the same. There is a chamber that holds the ground meat, which feeds down to the hole at the base, facing forward from a protruding thread. Nozzles are attached to this thread and secured with a collar. Above the chamber there is a cylinder piston, which is wound down into the chamber by turning the handle, forcing the meat downward. The piston must fit snugly into the chamber so that all the mix is forced down through the nozzle and into a skin.

Prosciutto on the meat slicer

To ensure a cool operation, you should immerse the parts of the sausage stuffer in ice water before use (as for a meat grinder, see p. 45). Most tabletop sausage stuffers have a clamp so they can be securely fixed to the work surface and won't move around when you apply pressure. I often think about inventing a musical version of a hand-cranked sausage stuffer, but I'm not sure if there's a market for it.

Different nozzles work for different products. The largest one is used for haggis and large salami, such as mortadella. The medium nozzle works for most salami and large sausages, while the smaller one is reserved for thin sausages, such as *chipolatas* and pepperoni. The nozzle should be matched with the right casings (see p. 86), which are fed onto it.

Meat slicer

This piece of equipment will probably be the one you use the least, and it is expensive. Expect to pay around $250 for a small domestic one and up to $1,700 for something more heavy-duty. But when it comes to creating wafer-thin slices of ham, bacon, pastrami, or *bresaola*, there is no substitute. The slicer plays no part in the making of the product but helps deliver it to the plate in its very best, most delicious form. It's the charcuterie equivalent of a stretch limo to the premiere. It can also tackle pieces of meat too hard to cut with even the sharpest knife.

The main consideration, other than cost and storage, is the range and size of products you will need to slice. If you will be making only a range of salami, for example, you will need only a small, vertical flatbed slicer. A larger version of this model would also allow you to cut meats such as a boned ham or pastrami, as well as cured, boned pieces such as bacon and prosciutto. For a large piece of meat such as *spalla* or *speck* (see p. 184), you would probably need to invest in a model with a supporting grip to hold the meat in place during operation.

A robust, gravity-fed slicer is the all-singing, all-dancing version that will have a large blade and the choice of belt or gear transmission. Belt transmission is functional and silent, whereas gear transmission allows you to calibrate the effort needed for the job in hand.

As with all equipment that has moving parts with the capacity to cut things, it is important to adhere to safe practice. Don't operate a meat slicer until you have read the instructions and fully understood how it works. Make sure the machine is standing on a flat, fixed surface, and always have the protective guard or hopper in place. It's best, I think, to be ever so slightly scared every time you come to use a meat slicer. This will prevent you from becoming cavalier and will make sure you totally focus on the job at hand.

These machines are substantial and not cheap, but they can quickly turn a keen amateur into a seasoned professional. The improved results you get are significant. As with all machinery, cleanliness is vital (see p. 54).

Knives and accessories

You could get by without some of the big machinery early on in your curing journey, but you will need a small set of knives and a few accessories from the start. From basic preparation through curing and eventually air-drying, these items of equipment are indispensable.

Knives

There is a vast array of knives on the market, which can seem bewildering, but you should need only a couple for curing and smoking at home. There is no need to spend a fortune on blades that have been forged and folded hundreds of times so that they are more akin to a samurai sword than a kitchen knife. You can buy good knives suited to a specific task for a reasonable price. I recommend a boning knife (curved or straight) and a chef's knife.

A boning knife designed for use with meat will have a thin blade with a small amount of flex and a sharp point, which is used to remove muscle from a joint. It will withstand constant contact with bone while allowing you to work in tight areas, such as the gap between a ball and socket joint in a pork shoulder, without damaging the meat. A boning knife for fish or poultry has much more flex in the blade and is not suitable for red meat.

A chef's knife has a long blade and is mostly used for cutting up large pieces of meat – for instance, so they will fit into a grinder. These knives are also perfect for cutting slices and steaks from raw or cooked meat.

Sharpening steel

A sharpening steel will help you keep a reasonably sharp knife sharp. It will not put an edge on a blunt knife; you would need a whetstone or professional knife sharpener to do that. A steel will extend the life of your blades. By passing a knife along the full length of the steel at an acute angle on both sides, you will keep an edge to it from tip to heel. I prefer to use a steel that is slightly oval in cross section, rather than completely round.

You should consider the condition of your knife before buying a steel. If the blade was sharp to begin with but has become dull, use a coarse-cut steel to get an edge back on it. If your knife is in good condition already, then a medium-cut steel will maintain it.

Butcher's saw

This piece of equipment will allow you to cut through bones quickly and efficiently. It is very similar to an ordinary hacksaw. The blade can be removed for cleaning and is replaceable when it loses its edge.

Butcher's saw and pork belly

Almost everyone I know has a hacksaw hanging in the shed or garage, and I understand the temptation to buy a new blade for it and just make do with that. I would advise against this; a new hacksaw won't cost you much, and it's far better to have one fit for the job. Keep the old one for tinkering with on DIY days.

Trays, boxes, and brine bins

Food-grade trays are usually made from plastic and are designed to keep food in the best possible condition. Often they have embossed images of a crossed knife and fork to indicate that they are rated "food grade." They are extremely useful for curing meat in because they are hygienic and don't react with salt, unlike an aluminium bowl. They are very easy to come by, cheap, and produced in many sizes. You will need a selection if you intend to dry cure or brine any meat or fish.

You can, however, get by without these trays via a little clever redeployment of the salad drawers in your fridge. Empty these drawers, give them a thorough cleaning, and put them back in place. Rename them "curing boxes" and enjoy the eureka moment, knowing that those newly acquired bits of equipment will allow you to cure everything from bacon to pastrami via *bresaola*, *coppa*, and pancetta.

Food-grade trays and salad-drawer curing boxes can hold only small pieces of meat, and at some point I hope you will want to create a significant salted, air-dried chunk of cured meat such as a prosciutto ham from a fine pork leg (see recipe on p. 156). In this case, you will need to invest in a couple of boxes, similar to the tray mentioned above but with much deeper sides and big enough to accommodate a whole leg and a considerable amount of salt.

In the past, I was a stickler for using wooden boxes – large wine boxes or pine boxes – but it was proven to me by my good friend Mark Diacono (writer, gardener, broadcaster) that plastic food-grade boxes actually work just as well, if not better. These boxes also double as brine bins that can hold a significant amount of liquid and big pieces of meat.

Butcher's block

A butcher's block is not the unproductive procrastination process of someone in the meat trade with a looming deadline. It is an important work area where you will do most of your meat processing.

If you are only ever going to work with small pieces of meat, an ordinary, sturdy wooden cutting board will probably suffice. But as soon as you graduate to large pieces or whole carcasses, or if you expect to be butchering fairly often, it is really important to have a large, designated work surface.

There are variously sized professional blocks, but even the smallest – at around 20 inches square – are neither portable nor cheap. You have to view a butcher's block for what it is: a beautifully constructed permanent fixture – and an investment

PDV salt and large food-grade box

Prices start in the region of $1,200, and most blocks require a supporting aluminum stand, too; you could even commission a custom-made block suited to your situation. The wood must be treated with oil and cleaned only with a wire brush, which takes the surface off like a planer. Water only serves to crack and ruin it.

I much prefer wooden boards to plastic ones. Wood has a better feel and also inherent antibacterial qualities. After a period of popularity for plastic blocks, the commercial sector is now favoring wood again, too.

Butcher's string and hooks

These items are extremely useful for all charcuterie and *salumi*. Proper butcher's string allows you to tie large cuts as well as help a salami retain its shape. And stainless steel hooks make hanging your products easy and secure.

Jambon sac/cheesecloth

A jambon sac and cheesecloth are used for the same purpose: to tie around meat to protect it while it is air-drying. A jambon sac is akin to a pillowcase – as the 100 percent cotton bag billows out, the air flows freely around the meat, helping to dry it out as well as allowing the natural yeasts and molds in the air to colonize its surface. You can see through the cloth to monitor any changes in the meat's condition. A sack fashioned from cheesecloth or muslin can be used in its place.

Meat safe

A meat safe is essentially a box with sides made of window screen, held together by a wooden frame with one side hinged as a door, in which you can cure meats. You can easily construct one at home, or look for one at a garage sale or junk shop.

Measuring tools

It is important to monitor the progress of your products throughout the curing process and also to make sure that the conditions you are keeping them in are favorable. The following instruments are a great reassurance.

Brinometer

Also known as a hydrometer or salinometer, this instrument will inform you how salty a brine is. A brinometer has a calibrated scale marked along its length. It sits vertically in the brine, resembling a glass fishing float, and the salinity is shown by how high the meter floats in the brine. It isn't an essential component of your tool kit – especially if you use measured quantities of salt and liquid – but it is useful for checking simple brines (see pp. 112–13).

Butcher's string

Butcher's hook

Muslin jambon sac

Brinometer

Kitchen Scale

Weights in both pounds and ounces are expressed with decimal points rather than fractions for greater accuracy, so you will need a digital, rather than analog (mechanical), scale. The scale must include gradations to two decimal places and must ideally also accommodate items of up to 22 pounds (10 kg).

pH measure

This device allows you to measure the acidity of your curing products, in order to ensure the correct level is maintained. It is particularly useful when making salami or fermented sausage, where the pH is crucial (see p. 107). There are several ways to attain the correct pH, but it is very reassuring to be able to double-check it accurately. Electronic pH readers have a probe, which you insert into the meat. You can also use pH strips, but these are a little less precise.

Thermo-hygrometer

This will allow you to monitor the relative humidity – the relationship between water content and temperature in the air – in the place you designate for air-drying. A simple wall-mounted version will do the trick. You can alter the humidity by increasing the flow of air or by using a humidifier or dehumidifier. A bowl of heavily saturated saltwater will also help raise humidity in the surrounding area if required.

Cleaning your equipment

Checking that your equipment is clean should be your first action before starting a recipe, and cleaning your equipment should be your last to ensure that you are operating within the best food safety, health, and hygiene parameters. Every moving part of machines – blades, plates, knives, nozzles, handles, and hoppers – should be scrupulously cleaned after use. Dismantle all moving parts of machines and either put through a dishwasher on a hot wash (above 150°F) or hand wash in a sink with a soap detergent, then allow to cool completely before reassembling. Don't put the plastic nozzles of your sausage stuffer in the dishwasher, however, because they are liable to become brittle and break. Instead, use a bottle brush to clean them after soaking in hot soapy water.

If you've got a butcher's block, do not soak it in water to clean it. Use only the recommended block brush that acts like a wood sander, stripping away the top surface of wood after every use.

Hanging salami before air-drying

Ingredients

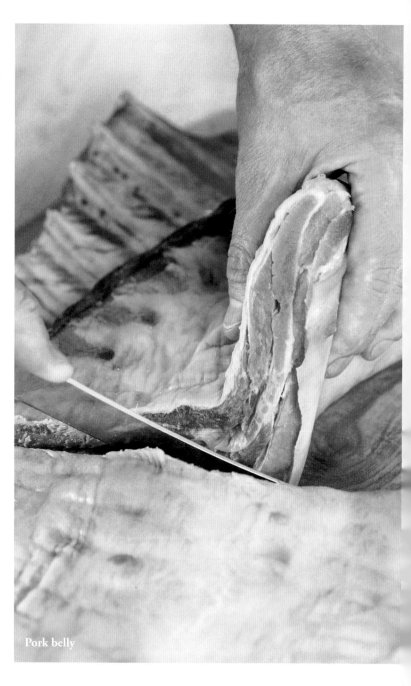

Pork belly

Curing and smoking are not techniques to disguise inferior

ingredients. They are ways to turn something good into an elevated version of itself. If you start with the best possible ingredients, you will get the best possible results. The trick is to use the methods to enhance an ingredient without losing its original flavors. They are adaptable techniques that can work their magic across almost anything, from meat and fish to cheese and vegetables.

Meat

In the following pages, you will find tables that list various cuts of pork, beef, lamb, and venison and the different curing techniques that work well on them. These are by no means exhaustive but offer a sound general overview that relates specifically to the recipes in this book.

First, a word on buying your meat. At River Cottage we are lucky enough to be able to use whole carcasses – the majority of which are reared on our farm – and there is a definite economy of scale here. We can create many different cured products at a time because we can utilize every part of the carcass. Buying small, individual pieces is fine, especially when you are first experimenting with curing. But if you can buy a half or whole carcass – or even use your own animals – it will certainly work out to be better value in the long run.

Initially, buying a lot of meat in one go might seem daunting. But you don't have to use it all at once. In fact, it may be advantageous not to do so. It is one of life's peculiarities that meat that has been previously frozen cures exceptionally well (ironic, when you consider that curing came about in the first place because refrigeration was not available). Preserving meat is all about drawing out the moisture, which is exactly what happens when you allow frozen meat to thaw – water drains away and fibers open up. So buying in bulk and then freezing some of your meat is a great start to curing success.

Of all the types of meat you would possibly cure from a whole carcass or large cuts, pork is the most likely. It is so versatile and accessible. Of course, not everyone will be in the position to buy and use a whole carcass, but this doesn't matter. The range of possibilities for turning pork into something cured is so extensive that even if you buy just one cut of pork, you have the option to turn it into several different things. It gives you choices and therefore it is an important ingredient in building your repertoire and furthering your knowledge.

As pork accounts for a large portion of the recipes in this book, I thought it would be useful to include some basic butchery techniques (see pp. 62–75) so that you can prepare cuts of pork ready to turn into all of the products listed in the table on p. 61.

Pork

The pig is the source of most of the well-known and celebrated cured goods. It is considered to be the original curing ingredient, particularly in the realms of charcuterie and *salumi*, although perhaps wild boar should really hold that title. Pork has a perfect ratio of fat to lean meat, and it responds favorably to all sorts of curing techniques.

We are extremely good at producing pork in Britain and have some of the highest welfare standards in the world. In terms of curing and smoking, it is only really bacon that is widely recognized as a typical British cured product. But that does not reflect the true potential of this meat, as you'll discover once you start dipping into the recipes.

You can learn everything you need to know about dry curing, brines, molds, and smoking with a small, inexpensive piece of pork. A sirloin cut is the perfect practice piece – ideal to experiment with until your adventures in curing and smoking take you further afield.

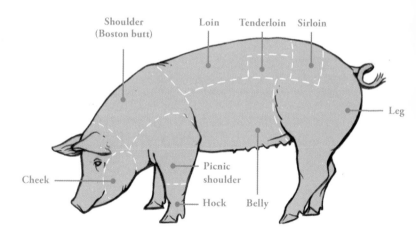

CUT	PRODUCT	TECHNIQUE	RECIPE
Picnic shoulder	Salami	Fermentation, air-drying	p. 167
	Chorizo	Fermentation, air-drying	p. 171
	Cotechino	Fermentation, air-drying	p. 175
	Hunter's sausage	Fermentation, cold smoking, air-drying	p. 235

CUT	PRODUCT	TECHNIQUE	RECIPE
Cheek	Guanciale	Dry curing, air-drying	p. 182
Shoulder (Boston butt)	Spalla	Dry curing, air-drying	p. 184
	Speck	Dry curing, cold smoking, air-drying	p. 184
	Salami	Fermentation, air-drying	p. 167
	Coppa	Dry curing	p. 152
	Chorizo	Fermentation, air-drying	p. 171
	Cotechino	Fermentation, air-drying	p. 175
	Hunter's sausage	Fermentation, cold smoking, air-drying	p. 235
Hock	Terrine	Wet curing, air-drying, cold smoking	p. 239
Loin	Canadian bacon	Dry curing	p. 142
	Chorizo	Fermentation, air-drying	p. 171
	Sichuan-cured pork	Dry curing, air-drying	p. 178
Belly	Bacon	Dry curing	p. 138
	Pancetta	Dry curing–brine hybrid, air-drying	p. 145
Sirloin	Cured sirloin	Total immersion method, air-drying	p. 159
		Wet curing, cold smoking	p. 195
Leg	Prosciutto	Total immersion method, air-drying	p. 156
	Cider-cured ham	Wet curing, air-drying, cold smoking (optional)	p. 195
Tenderloin	Filletto	Dry curing, air-drying	p. 178
	Hot smoked	Dry curing, hot smoking	p. 218
Fatback	Lardo	Dry curing	p. 151
Flare fat	Rendered	Confit (as for duck fat)	p. 207

Skinning and boning a picnic shoulder

If you want to use the hock to make a terrine (p. 239), then saw it off the joint at this point.

To prepare the picnic shoulder for grinding for making salami (pp. 167–68), chorizo (pp. 171–73), *cotechino* (pp. 175–76), or hunter's sausage (p. 235), place it, skin side down, on a cutting board or butcher's block and remove the small section of flat ribs from the underside and hock (pic 1). Reserve these to use for stocks and sauces.

To remove the skin, turn the hock so that the end where the trotter was is now facing toward you with the skin uppermost. Insert the knife all the way in between the skin and the flesh and then rotate it through 90 degrees so that the sharp edge is now pointing upward underneath the skin. Keeping the fingers of your holding hand away from the knife, lift the knife so that it cuts through the skin all the way to the top of the joint (pic 2).

Remove the skin by running the blade underneath the skin and pulling it away carefully with your free hand (pic 3); it should come off in one sheet. The skin can be put on top of a soup or stew (it will partially render and thicken it).

Starting at the knuckle end (pic 4), cut around the elbow joint to release it from the meat (pic 5) so that it can be pulled free (pic 6). The meat can now be cut into chunks, small enough to push through the grinder.

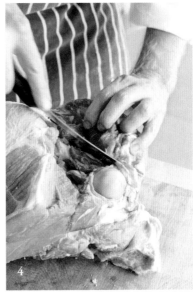

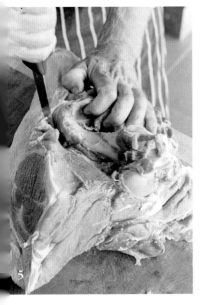

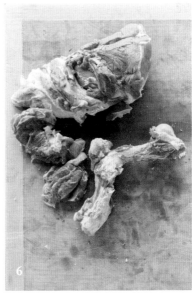

Boning a shoulder of pork

Place the shoulder, skin side down, on a cutting board or butcher's block so that you can clearly see the short row of top ribs and the spine extending into the neck bone. Slide the tip of the knife behind the top of the ribs and begin to separate the bone from the flesh using controlled strokes, keeping the knife close to the bones (pic 1). This will ensure you keep as much meat on the shoulder as possible. Follow the shape of the bone all the way down, using your other hand to pry the meat and bone apart (pic 2) until it is completely removed (pic 3). This bone can be kept for making a stock.

Locate the bone socket that protrudes from the meat. This is the blade bone. The blade bone can be quite tricky to remove because it has a flat side and a ridged side. With the shoulder still skin side down, the upper surface of the blade bone will be the flat side. Insert the knife just above the bone socket and cut along the flat bone to release the meat (pic 4), again using your free hand to gently pry open the meat (pic 5, p. 66).

Trace around the outline of the bone and then run the knife underneath, keeping it as close to the bone as you can (pic 6, p. 66). If you release the socket end of the bone first, you can lift it enough so that you can see underneath the bone, paying particular attention to the raised ridge in the middle (pic 7, p. 66). Navigate around the ridge as best you can and then remove the bone completely (pic 8, p. 66). At this point, the shoulder is ready to cure into *spalla* or *speck* (pp. 184–87).

If you wanted to mince the meat for salami (pp. 167–68), chorizo (pp. 171–73), *cotechino* (pp. 175–76), or hunter's sausage (p. 235), you would remove the outer layer of skin (rind) at this point and cut the meat into small enough chunks to pass through the grinder.

To remove the eye of meat that is cured to make *coppa* (p. 152), turn the shoulder so that it is facing you sideways on, with the "head end" away from you. You should be able to easily identify a seam of connecting tissue just to the side of the large round eye of meat. Insert the knife and work it along this seam, rolling back the meat as you go (pics 9–11, p. 67), until eventually it is removed (pic 12, p. 67)

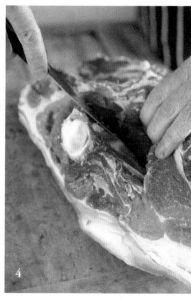

(continued on next page)

Boning a shoulder of pork (continued)

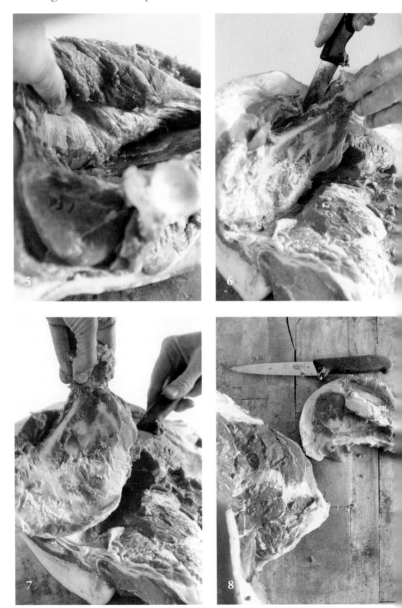

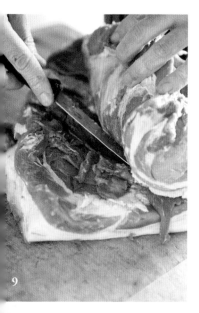

9

10

11

12

Boning a loin of pork

Lay the pork loin, skin side down, on a board or butcher's block so the spine and ribs are visible. The long triangular bone attached to the top of the ribs at the spine end is the chine. Saw horizontally under the length of the chine (pic 1) with a butcher's saw, taking care as you will be cutting toward your other hand. As it is released, hold the tail end of the bone out of the way (pic 2). Once the chine is removed, the other ends of the ribs are exposed and the loin is ready to make Canadian bacon.

For Sichuan-cured pork loin on p. 178, you will need to remove the bone from the eye of the meat. Insert the tip of the knife between the end of the ribs and the meat at one end (pic 3) and then follow the shape of the bone until your knife exits at the bottom end (pic 4). Then start to separate the top of the ribs from the meat along the length (pic 5). Keep the knife as close to the bone as possible (so as not to leave much meat on it) and use repeated strokes until the whole sheet of ribs and spine can be removed (pic 6). The ribs could be grilled or used in a stock.

To make *lardo*, you need to remove the fat from the meat in a nice thick slab (see recipe, p. 151). The fat will probably have a visible seam, which you can use as a guide to cut along. This is best done when the loin is still chilled and the fat is firm.

Boning a belly of pork

To prepare the belly for bacon, you need to remove any flaps of meat on the flesh side and make the cut edges clean and straight (pic 1). This will make the surfaces relatively flat, which is beneficial for this method, as you want the cure to act evenly. If there are flaps of meat or pockets of fat, the cure may not get underneath them and you will have areas that are not directly affected by the action of the cure mix.

If your piece of pork belly contains a section of rib bones, you can leave them in, as the cure will penetrate through them. Remove them only if you are proficient with the knife and feel confident that you can remove the bones in one sheet without leaving an undulating surface underneath where the bones sat. If you are left with peaks and troughs, as opposed to a flat surface, the cure mix will sit in the troughs and cause the cure to act in a less than uniform manner.

If you do decide to remove the rib bones from the belly, insert the knife at one end and work the blade relatively flat along the bones and as close as possible to them to cut the ribs free from the meat (pic 2).

There is no difference in the curing times if the bones are removed, or in fact if the piece of belly contained no bones in the first place.

More often than not, if the belly does have a section of rib bones, there will also be an elongated strip of meat and connective tissue running along the bottom edge. This formed part of the diaphragm of the pig and creates a flap that should be removed. Simply cut it right back at the base along its length (pic 3) and remove. The meat from this flap can be retrieved, ground, and used in any of the recipes originating from the shoulder or picnic shoulder and hock.

There may be a section of flare fat (see p. 81) on the inside. Unless the flare fat is much thicker than the meat or is misshapen, creating an uneven surface, you shouldn't need to remove it. If you do need to remove it, this is easily done by simply pulling it away from the flesh with your hand as if it were stuck on with Velcro.

Your prepared pork belly is now ready for curing (pic 4).

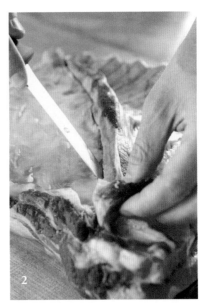

Preparing a belly of pork for pancetta

There are similarities between preparing pork belly for pancetta and the method for bacon, but with the added requirement to remove the outer rind and rib bones for pancetta. The belly is left flat for bacon, but a traditional pancetta is boned and rolled after it has been cured, so the removal of any bones is critical, and the rind is removed, so the hard skin isn't tucked into the middle of the rolled pancetta (see pp. 145–48).

The technique for adding the cure for both of these methods also differs and the preparation of the belly reflects this. With bacon, the cure isn't measured; instead it is applied liberally over 5 days and the liquid is removed each day. With pancetta, a measured amount of salt is added to the cure, which is in direct relation to the weight of the pork belly (once the rind and bones are removed), and it is applied only once. The liquid isn't removed but allowed to envelop the belly like a brine for a period of 3 days for every 1 pound (500g) boneless, rindless belly.

To remove the rib bones for pancetta, place the belly, rind side down, and run the tip of the knife between the rib bones and the connecting flesh. Keep the knife relatively flat and against the bones to keep as much meat on the belly as possible. This way the surface of the meat should remain flat and even. Lift the sheet of bones up out of the way with your free hand (pic 1), like opening a book until the bones are just connected at the base, which runs diagonally across the belly. It should now be easy to run the knife along the bottom of the bones to remove them.

If there are any large pieces of flare fat that create an uneven surface, remove them. Sometimes the flare fat covers the whole underside of the belly, particularly if it is from the part of the belly toward the back leg. If it is fairly level, there is no need to remove it.

Turn the belly over so that it is flat on a surface with the rind uppermost. Insert the knife just under the rind and score around the edges (pic 2). In a similar fashion to the removal of the rib bones, use your spare hand to pull back the rind (pic 3) so that you leave as much fat on the belly as you can. If possible, the rind should be thin and almost transparent. Once removed, it can be slashed and salted for crackling or used to thicken a soup or stew by placing it on the top.

Once the bones and rind have been removed, the meat is ready to have the cure applied. If the piece of belly is quite big, you may have to trim off one edge (pic 4) so that it will fit your vacuum or ziplock bag. Or get a bigger bag!

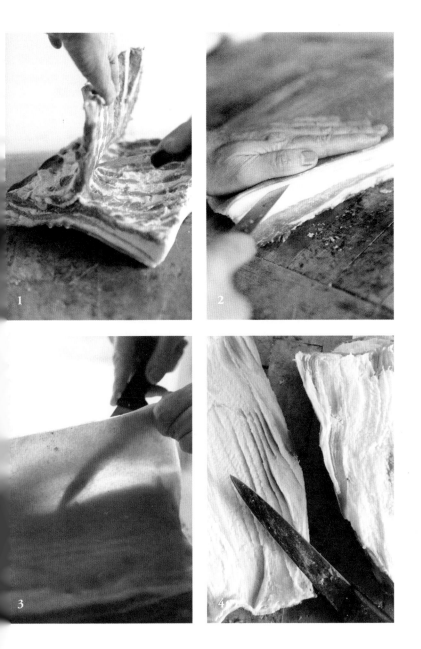

Boning a leg of pork

With all joints of meat being prepared for curing, you should remove any flaps of skin, meat, or fat that will obstruct the cure mix penetrating evenly and successfully. This is also true of the leg. If there are any flaps, they will more often than not be around the exposed meat at the top of the leg and should be cut off so that the surface area is flat.

Traditionally the aitchbone is removed before curing a whole leg, whether it is a prosciutto, Ibérico, or Parma ham (see p. 156). The first time you cure a whole leg, you should leave this bone on because it is quite a tricky operation to remove it until you have improved your knife skills. Also, if you keep it on, then you are protecting the area around the femur bone underneath, which can cause a problem if it isn't salted well enough. The only adverse issue with leaving the aitchbone on is that it also acts as a barrier when you come to slice the ham once it is cured. So you do have to take it off eventually, and although it is a bit tricky to do, it is more straightforward to remove it before the ham is cured because it is easier to get the knife around the bone when the meat is soft and fresh, as opposed to hard and rigid.

To remove the aitchbone, locate it and feel for the raised ridge running along it. Grab this ridge with your free hand; it will enable you to pull the bone away from the flesh once you have made some initial cuts, as well as keep your free hand out of the way of the knife during this slightly tricky procedure. Remove any meat that is sitting on top of the aitchbone (pic 1) so you can clearly see the shape and then trace the outline with the tip of the knife (pic 2).

Start to work the knife underneath the bone, which is fairly flat apart from the ridge that you hold until you can see the socket that has the "ball" of the femur bone connected to it (pic 3). The ball and socket are connected by ligaments that you have to cut in order for the aitchbone to be removed. Get your knife in between the ball and socket and cut through the ligaments. Once this has been done, you can work away at the rest of the meat so that you can eventually remove the whole aitchbone like a cap (pic 4).

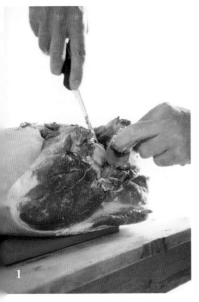
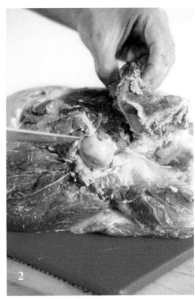

Beef

Beef is associated with British food heritage much more than pork is, though it isn't linked with traditional British curing techniques. This seems strange when you consider that we are all comfortable with the notion of well-hung, aged beef. But we have to look further afield for curing and smoking recipes that use beef. I think it makes sense to choose cuts of meat that we would traditionally use for a roast or slow roast and apply a new European slant to them.

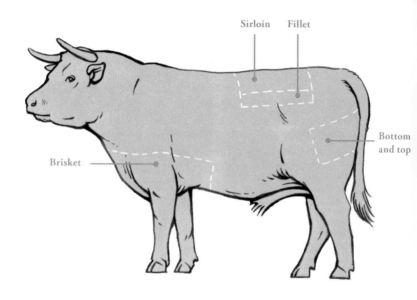

CUT	PRODUCT	TECHNIQUE	RECIPE
Bottom round or top round	Bresaola	Dry curing, wet curing, air-drying	p. 190
Brisket	Pastrami	Dry curing–brine hybrid, air-drying, cold smoking	p. 233
	Salt beef	Wet curing	p. 200
Boned sirloin or fillet	Hot smoked rose-cured beef	Dry curing, hot smoking	p. 216

Lamb

I love the sweet tenderness of lamb, but one of my pet peeves is cold lamb fat, which is a bit of an obstacle when it comes to curing. The fat from lamb – known as tallow when rendered – was traditionally used in candles and soap – perfect applications for it, in my opinion. There is also little or no fat marbling within lamb meat (unlike beef, say), so it can be a bit tricky to cure and is something of an acquired taste. However, the recipes listed below work really well, particularly if you use meat from a sheep in its second year.

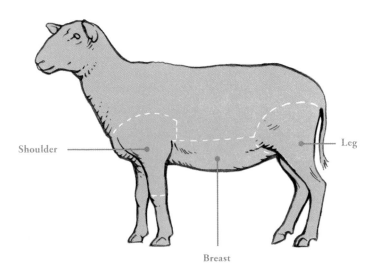

CUT	PRODUCT	TECHNIQUE	RECIPE
Leg	Culatello	Dry curing–wet curing hybrid, air-drying	p. 192
	Oak-smoked spiced lamb	Marinade, grill hot smoking	p. 229
	Lamb violin	Dry curing, air-drying	p. 165
Shoulder	Pine-smoked merguez	Cold smoking	p. 236
Breast	Lambcetta	Dry curing–brine hybrid, air-drying	p. 147

Goat

Goat is very underrated as a meat but has wonderful gamy flavors when cured. It can be used to make exceptional salami when mixed with pork to up the fat ante, and the violin recipe illustrates a very traditional method of curing a leg.

CUT	PRODUCT	TECHNIQUE	RECIPE
Leg	Goat violin	Dry curing, air-drying	p. 164

Game

As a lean meat, venison is perhaps not the obvious choice for curing, but in fact there are various traditional recipes for it. In and around Scandinavia, elk and moose are used in salami, and, of course, standard *biltong* has springbok meat as its base, all of which share similar characteristics to venison.

CUT	PRODUCT	TECHNIQUE	RECIPE
Venison haunch	Biltong	Dry curing, wet curing, air-drying	p. 188

Duck

Duck has a wonderful covering of fat and takes very well to curing. You can use either wild or farmed duck breasts to make a simple duck prosciutto by following the principles of a traditional dry cured ham, or hot smoke them using tea leaves and cedar plank.

CUT	PRODUCT	TECHNIQUE	RECIPE
Breast	Prosciutto	Dry curing, air-drying	p. 183
	Cedar smoked	Dry curing, hot smoking	p. 226
Leg	Confit	Dry curing, confit	p. 207

Fish

Both oily and white fish cure well and are perhaps more accessible and less daunting than large joints of meat. Fish was probably the first ingredient to be smoked and takes to this form of curing particularly well. I like to keep the flavor of the smoke quite subtle, so that the taste of the fish isn't lost in the process. There are endless possibilities, and I am yet to be disappointed with any fish I have smoked. Many wonderful dishes are created with smoked fish, such as kedgeree and chowder.

FISH	PRODUCT	TECHNIQUE	RECIPE
Pollack	Cold smoked pollack	Dry curing, cold smoking	p. 241
Salmon	Gravlax	Dry curing–brine hybrid	p. 154
	Smoked fillets in prosciutto	Dry curing, hot smoking	p. 225
Mackerel	Hot smoked mackerel	Dry curing, hot smoking	p. 212
Sea bream	Smoked fillets in prosciutto	Dry curing, hot smoking	p. 225
Mussels	Pine-smoked mussels	Hot smoking	p. 220
Oysters	Hot smoked oysters	Hot smoking	p. 223

Cheese and vegetables

There is little or no preparation needed to smoke cheese and vegetables: you simply put the ingredient in a cold (or sometimes hot) smoker and allow it to take on those flavors over a few hours.

Oak-smoked Cheddar (see p. 243) is a familiar product and this can be made at home. Note that with thick-rinded cheeses, it is better to remove the rind so the smoke can fix itself to the surface. But you can cold smoke soft cheeses such as Brie and Camembert, too. I particularly love the flavor of a ripe, creamy Brie lightly smoked over beech or apple wood. You can also hot smoke cheese (see variation, p. 227) by soaking a cedar plank in water and using it inside a kettle grill.

When it comes to smoking vegetables, the possibilities are endless. Garlic is more exotic once smoked, while cold smoked potatoes take on an extra dimension in a summer salad (see p. 244). Tomato puree can be hot smoked, then spiked with cold smoked chiles for a double whammy of smokiness.

You can also smoke your own herbs and spices, such as the paprika that gives chorizo its distinctive edge. The way to achieve all of these smoky herbs and spices is to lay a small piece of cheesecloth in the bottom of a colander or sieve and place the herb or spice on top of it in a cold smoker. The cheesecloth is fine enough to stop the ingredients from falling through but will allow the smoke to waft up through the colander and flavor the herbs and spices.

You could smoke your own black pepper and salt as well, which would add a smoky note to anything you cure. Herbs and spices can be cold smoked for several hours, depending on how intense you want the flavor to be.

Rendering fat

Fat

In terms of curing and smoking, pork fat is the king. It is a rich source of flavor, it replaces some of the moisture lost in the drying process, and it also acts as a protective barrier, allowing the curing process to take place over a longer period of time, which in turn helps flavor to develop further. There are several types of pork fat. You are unlikely to be able to buy any of these in a supermarket, but a good butcher will always prepare some for you.

Fatback This is the thick layer of firm fat found just below the rind running along the loin and around the shoulder. It's the fat that borders the meat in a slice of Canadian bacon. It is also removed and cured in sheets for the classic Italian specialty, *lardo*. Fatback can be used to fix flavor, texture, and moistness in salami, blood sausage, pâtés, and terrines. It can also be wrapped around lean meats like venison to stop them from drying out during cooking (a technique known as barding). As a commodity in the kitchen, fatback cannot be surpassed. It can be frozen and kept indefinitely.

Flare fat or belly fat This is an internal fat that lines the belly of a pig. It is softer than fatback and is present in bacon. It is often found with striations of meat in it and is considered less pure than fatback, but its meatiness can be used to advantage in some products. Belly fat is easy to remove from the belly and can be pulled off in sheets as if it were stuck on with Velcro. I sometimes add flare fat to sausages, but I find the best use of it is to render it to lard (as you would duck fat, see p. 207) for confits.

Leaf lard fat During the slaughtering process, the lungs, liver, heart, and spleen of the animal, collectively known as the "pluck," are removed. These would spoil very quickly if left in place. The only organs left in the carcass are the kidneys because they are protected by leaf fat, also known as "flead." It is comparable to beef suet that surrounds beef kidneys. This fat is thick and brittle and is considered by many to be the best fat for making pastry, although in curing terms it would probably be rendered for a confit.

Caul fat This membrane that lines the stomach and intestines of the pig looks like fine lace. It can be used to line terrines or as a replacement for sausage skins, or it can be wrapped around a lean cut such as a stuffed tenderloin, allowing the meat to keep its shape during the cooking process as well as browning and flavoring the surface. Caul fat should be soaked in water before use, to ensure it becomes as flexible as possible.

Salt

Salt comes in many varieties of differing quality. The two main methods by which salt is produced are mining from rocks and evaporation from seawater. Both methods have a long tradition. The latter is much older, although the Chinese began using wells to reach underground pools of saltwater two millennia ago.

Rock salt is simply crystallized salt, also known as halite. It is the result of the evaporation of ancient oceans that left large deposits, now deep underground. The process of getting rock salt to the table is more involved than that for sea salt. Rock salt is drilled out, then put through several crushing and grading sequence before it is sorted into size and bagged. Or it may be mixed in deep wells with fresh water under high pressure and pumped to the surface as brine, and then evaporated at a refinery.

Sea salt is the remains of evaporated seawater, either allowed to form naturally via the heat of the sun in large shallow salt pans, or artificially heated to a point where the crystals form and can be harvested. If every sea and ocean in the world evaporated, there would be enough salt to cover the whole of North and South America about a mile and a half deep.

As rock salt is more extensively processed, it is often considered to be a lesser product than sea salt. Specifications for salt vary widely according to the intended use. Salt destined for human consumption must be much purer than salt used for say, melting ice on a path or putting in your dishwasher.

For most purposes, salt can have a gray, pink, or brown tinge rather than being pure white. *Fleur de sel* (flower of salt) is regarded as one of the best-quality sea salts, and it often has a grayish tint to it, stemming from residual sand particles in the pans where it is evaporated. There is also a microscopic alga *Dunalia salina*, commonly found in salt marshes, that can give salt a light pink tint. This should not be confused with pink salt, which is salt premixed with additional nitrates and nitrites.

The highest-graded salts have a more complex mineral makeup than ordinary table salt, containing various amounts of sodium chloride, calcium, magnesium, iodine, iron, and potassium. Varying combinations of these contribute to the individual flavor of different salts. Certain minerals can cause problems – for example, calcium and magnesium both tend to make salt absorb more water, causing it to clump together, or "cake." Often an anticaking additive is mixed with the salt, such as sodium ferrocyanide 535, or a natural agent, such as magnesium carbonate, may be used.

At River Cottage, the salt we use for curing is "pure dried vacuum" (PDV) salt. Once the salt has been mined, it is turned into PDV salt by evaporating a brine a vacuum – a highly energy-efficient process because the brine boils at a lower temperature than the normal 212°F. As well as being 99.9 percent pure and affordable in large quantities, PDV salt granules are much finer than sea salt or rock salt. Under the microscope, they are cuboid in shape and all the grains are small and the same size. This means that they have an even effect on anything you are curing because the salt particles dissolve and penetrate at the same rate, giving a better overall cure. These small, even particles also lock together, creating a good covering for methods such as salt-box curing, which is used for large pieces of meat, like a leg of pork.

Sea salt is mostly formed of large crystals. They add fantastic flavor, texture, and looks to a finished meal but dissolve unevenly and don't lock together. At River Cottage, we mostly use this type of salt for seasoning or finishing off a dish rather than curing.

If you've followed other curing recipes, you will more than likely have come across different varieties of salt. In many recipes originating in the United States, kosher salt is often used and pink salt is sometimes used for curing. Kosher salt is a high-grade, large-crystal salt, usually free of any additives. The kosher tag refers to the fact that salt draws away any residual blood from the meat, in line with the rules for the preparation of kosher meat – the salt itself is not kosher. Pink salt is the collective term for synthetic curing mixes with added nitrites and nitrates such as cures #1 and #2 (see pp. 30–31).

Salt should always be weighed, not measured by volume, because different salt crystals vary in their mass. For example, sea salt has a greater mass than PDV salt, and so using the same volume of either would produce a different level of saltiness.

Sugars

Sugar is not an essential ingredient in curing, but it does have its role. It can be added to both dry and wet cures, and as well as contributing sweetness, it has anti-microbial qualities similar to those of salt. I prefer sugars such as Demerara and dark muscovado that retain some of their natural molasses, as this gives them a more robust flavor. Some Demerara sugars are just refined white sugar that's been dyed brown again, so make sure you source a good-quality Demerara.

You can also employ the sweetness of honey, maple syrup, or dark molasses in your cures, as is common in traditional bacon and baked ham recipes such as the cider-cured ham on p. 195. But, on the whole, I prefer to stick with the brown sugars. They work really well with pork and beef, and in brines for poultry. The only exception is in the classic gravlax cure (see p. 154), where I prefer to use some superfine sugar. Fish is much more delicate than meat and so a gentler sweetener is called for.

Herbs and spices for curing

Malt vinegar

I use malt vinegar to make the brine for *biltong* (p. 188) and for wiping the outside of hams and salami that I intend to air-dry. It is a natural sterilizer and raises the acidity level on the surface of the meat, helping attract the desirable mold.

Always use good-quality malt vinegar as opposed to "nonbrewed condiment," which is the vinegar substitute used at the local fish-and-chip shop. A by-product of the oil industry, it is nowhere near the quality of malt vinegar.

Herbs and spices

There is no limit to the additional ingredients you could use to flavor your cures, and this is an area where you can be really creative. But there are some traditional favorites that have stood the test of time for good reason, and it pays to be aware of these. For example, I wouldn't attempt to make chorizo without paprika, though I might add a slug of tequila instead of wine as a creative tweak.

I prefer to use fresh herbs because the flavors are more vibrant, but there is no shame in using dried herbs if that is all you have. I store fresh herbs like cut flowers, in a jar of water. If I need to keep them longer than a day, I wrap the bunch in a clean paper towel and put it in the salad drawer of the fridge. Dried spices do not keep indefinitely, as they lose their intensity. Keep them in sealed jars in a cool, dark cupboard and replace as necessary.

These are my favorite herbs and spices, with their key flavor characteristics:

Black pepper Spicy and pungent
White pepper Mild and musty
Mace Delicate, fragrant, and smooth
Nutmeg Like mace, but more bitter
Garlic Pungent, spicy, and sweet
Paprika Sweet, aromatic, spicy, and often smoky
Cilantro Sweet and floral
Juniper Bitter and dry
Sage Fragrant and piny
Bay Strongly aromatic, with a hint of spice
Thyme Fragrant and light
Fennel Freshly pungent, with a hint of licorice
Cayenne Hot and spicy
Tarragon Light anise flavor
Clove Christmassy

Casings

You can use synthetic casings that are spun from collagen for your sausages and salami, but I prefer natural casings made from animal intestines. Synthetic casings often have an inferior texture, and although they are perhaps easier to buy, they are often more expensive because they are sold with a ready-made cure mix containing nitrates and nitrites (see pp. 30–35).

Natural casings are put through a very stringent cleansing process before they are available for sale. They are stripped from the animal after slaughter, turned inside out, cleaned of their mucus membrane, turned back around, and packed in salt. Different casings suit different products. Sheep's intestines are narrow and are used to make *chipolata* sausages. Pig's intestines (pork "middles") are used for breakfast sausages or smaller salami, such as the hunter's sausage on p. 235. Beef "middles" and "rounds" are good for most salami (pp. 167–68), and beef "bung" is used for *cotechino* (pp. 175–76) and mortadella (p. 181).

Natural casings should be rehydrated before use to maximize their elasticity. Do not hold them under a running tap, as it will trap too much water in the skins, which will dilute the flavor of whatever you put in them. Instead you should just soak them in a bowl of cold water in advance of using them – a couple of hours should suffice. You can resalt unused casings and store them in the fridge or freezer.

Natural casings do split on occasion, but despite this slight annoyance, I still prefer their superior texture. To me, biting into a sausage in a synthetic casing feels like eating something still in its wrapper. Natural casings, unsurprisingly, blend more into the product and don't feel like a barrier to the meat inside. And, of course, they have a more traditional look to them. You'll probably notice an unpleasant smell when you first open the packet, but this soon disappears and doesn't carry through to the flavor of the meat you put in them. You can buy natural casings online or from your butcher.

Salted and rehydrated natural casings

Tied fresh salami

Filling and tying salami

Making salami is quite an operation and requires planning as well as preparation and some patience, but it is time well spent. The following method is the same for every salami you make, the only differences being the ingredients and length of maturing time.

I use natural casings for salami – normally beef round casing, which is the lower intestine of a steer. These need to be presoaked in cold water for about 2 hours. You will also need to cut several pieces of string, each about 6 inches long, ready to tie the end of the casings.

Grind the meat coarsely, using the coarse (⅓ to ⅜ inch) plate of your grinder, then mix it by hand with the correct ratios of salt and other ingredients, according to your chosen recipe.

Pack the mixture into the cleaned and cooled barrel of a sausage stuffer and place a medium nozzle on the end. Turn the handle so that any air trapped inside the barrel is released and you can see the salami mix filling the nozzle (pic 1, p. 90). Moisten the nozzle with a small amount of cold water. Open one end of a length of beef round casing and feed it onto the nozzle (pic 2, p. 90), leaving the casing end just hanging off (pic 3, p. 90).

Tie the end of the casing with string, using a simple knot and leaving some string hanging down (pics 4 and 5, pp. 90–91).

Now twist the ends of the string into a new knot. When the knot is pulled tight, the string will form a loop (pics 6 and 7, p. 91). The loop is important because it will make it easy to hang the salami for drying.

Push the casing back onto the nozzle. Fill the casing with the mixture to a length of 12 inches or so, taking care not to overfill it (pic 8, p. 91). Release any pockets of trapped air by pricking the skin with a sterilized pin or sausage pricker.

To secure the mix in the casing, tie a half-knot at the end of the sausage near the nozzle, using a second piece of string (pic 9, p. 92). Pull a short length of round off the nozzle.

Now tie a simple knot around the casing by the nozzle, using a third length of string. You will have a short length of empty casing between two knotted pieces of string (pic 10, p. 92). Cut the empty casing in the middle (pic 11, p. 92). Finish off the knot on the second piece of string (pic 12, p. 92) and create a loop as before.

Repeat the process with the remaining mixture.

Filling salami is something that you can easily do on your own, but it is a simpler job when you have someone helping, sharing the tasks of filling, tying, and hanging the finished salami.

Natural casings tend to bow into a horseshoe shape. I put the loops from both ends on one hook and hang them like this. However, if you hang them from one end only, they will straighten. It just depends on your aesthetic.

Filling and tying salami

(continued on next page)

Filling and tying salami (continued)

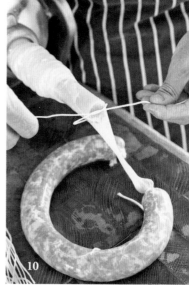

The salami should be hung initially in a warm place, at 77°F to 81°F. This will enable incubation of the bacteria to take place and facilitate fermentation. After 12 hours in this environment, move the salami to your dry curing spot, which should be between 50°F and 64°F, with a humidity level between 60 to 80 percent and a constant circulation of air. Make sure the salami are not touching a wall or one another and are not in direct sunlight.

Over the coming weeks, test the pH to ensure it is below 4.5. A white mold should form on the casings, indicating that this level has been reached.

The salami will take anywhere from 6 to 10 weeks to mature, depending on the conditions and the girth of the salami casing – the thicker the salami, the longer it takes to mature.

You can try the salami as soon as they are fairly firm to the touch and dry looking, but they will continue to dry out and harden until they are practically rock hard. The exception is 'nduja salami (p. 230), whose contents are eaten as a soft, spicy spread, taken from the salami at a much earlier stage.

When your salami reach the firmness you like, you can wipe off any mold from the outside with a cloth soaked in vinegar. This isn't essential, but not everyone is comfortable with the appearance of mold.

Serve your salami cut into slices, 1/16 to 1/18 inch thick. If you prefer, peel off the ring of casing from each slice before eating, although it is perfectly safe to eat.

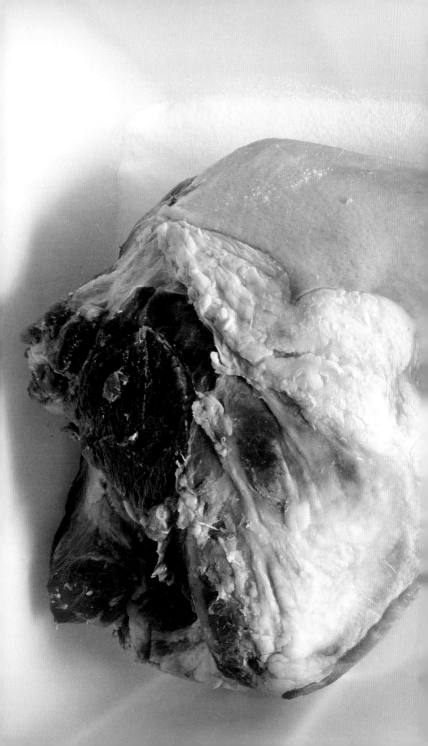

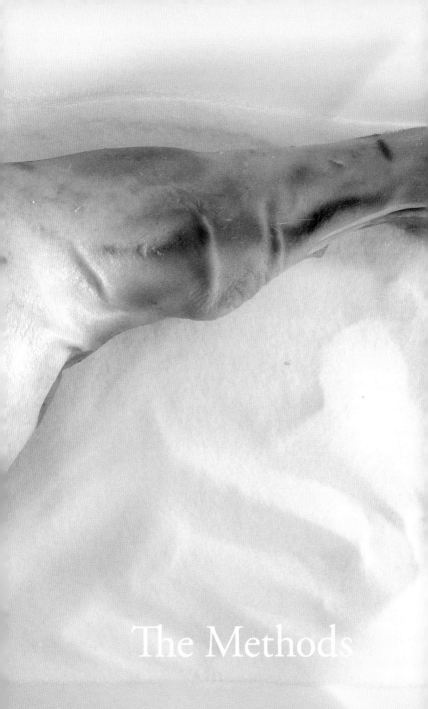

The Methods

Over the past decade, through a very enjoyable process o
trial and error, experimentation and success, I've learned the simplest and mos
effective ways to cure and smoke fresh meats and other foods. Those tried-and
tested methods are outlined here in detail so that whichever of my recipes yo
choose to try, you'll have all the information you need to achieve great results
Curing and smoking will expand your culinary horizons – often literally, as bi
quantities, capacious containers, and large pieces of equipment tend to be the orde
of the day. But, for the most part, the methods themselves are extremely simple.

Dry curing

This is one of the most accessible forms of preservation: you are simply applyin
salt to a piece of fresh meat.

We have come a long way from the days when our ancestors sailed uncharte
oceans to discover and claim for themselves "new" lands, their ships groaning wit
preserved food. To create supplies for their journey, they simply packed fresh me
and fish in great vats of salt. It would have tasted pretty awful, but it was edible.

These days, we no longer salt food out of necessity, and our methods are muc
more refined. Knowledge and experience have taught us the minimum amount o
salt required, and we've also learned to include other ingredients that have
positive effect on the products and also please the palate.

Curing should never be a way to mask the flavor of an inferior product, thoug
all too often it is. Take bacon, for example: it is such a common commodity, y
despite its potential to turn a vegetarian into a carnivore at a single sniff, it is rare
as good as it should be. I am sure we have all experienced inferior bacon, perha
bought from the corner shop on a Saturday morning, possibly under the influenc
of a slight hangover. It tends to have an oil-slick sheen to it and an inappropriate
short use-by date for something purporting to be cured. On cooking, the slic
shrink to half their original size and leach out a gray-white precipitation. It als
somehow retains the same color it had on removing it from the packet.

This is not how it should be. What you are getting in that packet is a pie
of pork that has been injected with a saline solution and some nonnatur
preservatives in order to keep it stable for the short period of time necessary to g
it from factory to shop to plate.

At River Cottage, we use a basic dry cure for our bacon. The mix consists o
equal quantities of PDV salt and Demerara sugar, to which we add finely choppe
bay leaves (usually fresh, but dried is okay) and some cracked black pepper. I als
like to add lightly bruised juniper berries (a favorite ingredient of mine) befo
mixing it all up. This simple cure delivers great results every time and is versati

Basic cure mix

enough to work with many products; it is a launch pad to more elaborate cures and methods. Use it as a simple and delicious way into curing and then, as you get more confident and experienced, you can try other techniques and ingredients.

Salt is the common denominator in dry curing, but there are different ways of applying it. You can measure out the salt in proportion to the weight of meat you are curing and leave the meat in contact with it for a set time. Alternatively, you can apply a smaller amount of fresh cure several times over a period of a week, tipping away the moisture drawn out of the meat on a daily basis.

You can also apply a dry cure once and allow it to turn into a brine without tipping the moisture away. Or, as in the case of a prosciutto or Parma-style ham, totally immerse a fine-quality leg of pork in a vast quantity of salt, remove it after a calculated period, and leave it hanging for a year or until it has lost 30 percent of its original weight.

Basic dry cure method

The basic dry cure technique works for both bacon and Canadian bacon (although because Canadian bacon is a thicker piece of meat, it takes longer to execute). consider this an entry-level method – not because it is inferior to other methods, but because you don't have to be too precise with weights and percentages, and yet the results are amazing and will boost your confidence. This method also allows you to see the effects of curing almost immediately because, on applying the cure, moisture will visibly begin to leach out of the pork, and over the course of just few days, the meat will become firmer and drier.

To make bacon, the cure mix is applied by hand to a piece of pork so that it has a liberal covering on all sides. It is then allowed to gently go about its business in food-grade tray placed in a domestic fridge. Liquid will pool in the tray, and you need to pour this away every day, as well as apply another liberal handful of cure each day until the curing period has been completed (5 days for bacon or 10 days for Canadian bacon). Less and less liquid will pool out each day until the salt cure has reached equilibrium with the meat. The texture of the meat will become firmer and the color darker – all telltale signs of the curing process in action. After the allotted curing time, you rinse off any residual cure from the meat and pat it dry with a clean tea towel. You then need to allow the bacon to mature and rest for the same number of days as you applied the cure to it, either back in your fridge or hanging in your designated air-drying spot (see p. 103).

Salt-box method

This is a step on from the basic dry curing method for bacon. The salt-box method is used when curing a whole muscle as for *coppa* (p. 152), or with pork tenderloin to get it ready for hot smoking (p. 218). The weight of the meat can vary, so it

Base layer of cure mix

impossible to give a precise amount of cure in the recipe. Instead, you coat the surface of the meat uniformly with cure and leave it for a particular length of time depending on the weight of the meat. A good rule of thumb is 1 day's curing fo every 2.2 pounds (1 kg) of meat.

You need to place all your cure ingredients in a food-grade tray (or wooden sal box, if you prefer) large enough to accommodate the meat while you are turning i in the cure. Make sure all the herbs and spices in your cure are evenly distribute throughout the salt. The cure ingredients don't need to be weighed, but the mea does. Place the meat (or fish) in the cure and turn it so that the entire surface i covered. The amount that adheres naturally to the surface of the meat will b sufficient to cure it. Whole muscles or boneless joints are not susceptible to harmfu bacteria or botulism, because bacteria cannot penetrate their interior. Air-dryin will complete this curing process.

A minimum of 2 percent salt to the weight of meat gives consistent success, an 5 percent is the maximum salt you can use in a dry cure before the result star to become unpalatable. Take into consideration that seawater on average has 3.5 percent salinity level. I tend to adhere to a 3 percent salt ratio.

Total immersion method

This method is used to produce prosciutto or Parma-style ham. It is one of th oldest and simplest of techniques, usually applied to a whole back leg of pork, prio to a period of air-drying. You can apply the same technique to a sirloin cut, whic is much smaller and therefore ready much sooner.

You need a lot of salt for this method because the meat must be completely burie in it. An average-size leg of pork takes at least 55 pounds (25 kg) of salt. That ma sound excessive, but it is necessary. The golden rule for curing a ham in this way is bury it in salt for 3 days per 2.2 pounds (1 kg) of meat. You should also apply weight, such as another, unopened sack of salt, placed on a cutting board on top the salted leg. This will help press moisture out of the buried ham. Unlike with oth dry curing, you won't need to empty the liquid; it will be absorbed into the salt.

Obviously, you need a pretty big box for this method, ideally big enough accommodate a whole leg with the trotter still attached. In the past, I have use boxes made from pine or large wine boxes. I like the look and feel of wood. Howeve plastic boxes actually have an advantage over wood because they are slight transparent and therefore it is easy to see if the salt isn't totally surrounding the l inside. You can then adjust the position of the leg so that the salt runs into any gap The other advantage of plastic boxes is that they are easy to clean and store.

Before you put your leg of pork in, you must weigh it so you can calculate t curing time and also determine when it has lost 30 percent of its original weig and is therefore ready to eat raw. The full recipe for this method is on pp. 156–5

Total immersion method

Air-drying *bresaola*

Air-drying

With all dry curing techniques, the application of the cure is only half the story. Once you have completed the salting stage, you still have to play the waiting game and allow the cure to mature the meat by air-drying. For some, this proves to be a psychological stumbling block because it can involve hanging meat not only outside of refrigeration but outside – literally.

It is perfectly possible to control or manipulate the conditions for air-drying cured meat without the need for expensive equipment. The three main factors are humidity, temperature, and flow of air. Creating the right environment could be as easy as finding a place out of direct sunlight, where the temperature is comfortable and a flow of air can move across the meat on a regular basis. Think porch or outbuilding, or a badly made shed or garage where the air can whistle through. Cellars can work as long as the air isn't stagnant. The meat must have a flow of air even if it means manufacturing it with a desk fan.

Of course, to minimize the risk of flies and to get the optimum humidity, temperature, and airflow, it is only really advisable to hang curing meat outside at the right time of the year. In the United Kingdom, the perfect conditions usually occur between October and the end of April. You are looking for

- temperatures of 50°F to 64°F,
- humidity of 60 to 80 percent (measured with a thermo-hygrometer), and
- constant flow of air.

If you just can't reconcile yourself to the fact that your meat will be left to its own devices outside, there are several ways in which you can "protect" it without negatively altering the process. You could use a jambon sac or cheesecloth wrapped loosely around it (see p. 52); if the cheesecloth is wrapped too tightly around the meat, it will still allow flies to lay eggs through it. You could also manufacture a meat safe (see p. 52), and I have known people to hang their hams in coarse fish keeping nets. As long as the mesh is small enough, your ham will not get fly eggs on it.

Even if you do get fly eggs on your ham or other cured meat, it isn't necessarily a problem. If you spot them in time (look for small, yellow-white clusters), you can easily just wipe them off with a cloth soaked in malt vinegar. A fly wants to lay eggs where it is wet and dark, so they won't always be in the most open place. If the eggs get to the next stage of development, then you have to confront maggots.

I have been curing hams like this for years and have had only two incidents with maggots. On the first occasion I was able to remove the small piece of the leg that contained the maggots and continued to air-dry the ham with great success. The second time, there was no rescuing the leg because the maggots had eaten through to the middle of it. The fly must have laid eggs on the ham even before it was packed in salt. Both hams were hung outside in early spring, so perhaps, in retrospect, I was pushing it a bit, season-wise. Such pitfalls can happen to anyone, but there are many things you can do to help prevent them.

If the idea of hanging meat outside in the right conditions still does not appeal to you, or if you want to cure meat year-round, you might need to invest in a bit of equipment or at least commandeer a fridge for curing purposes only. You needn't spend a fortune on a secondhand fridge, but you do need to use it only for curing and air-drying because it will be running at a higher temperature than a normal fridge, and any products that you cure in there will ultimately attract mold. This will travel across to other products, and although mold is ideal for curing, it isn't generally what you want on everything else in a normal fridge.

At River Cottage HQ, we have commercial curing fridges that enable us to control temperature and humidity. They also have large fans inside that turn air over the meat continuously. They are not very different from domestic fridges, except that they are much bigger. However, as soon as the weather conditions permit, we hang our cured products outside.

With a domestic fridge, you can set it to its warmest operating temperature for drying, around 50°F, though you wouldn't want to do this while there are other foods in it. Some modern fridges have different internal temperatures for different compartments, but they are not the norm.

Most fridges have an internal fan system as standard, so that air can circulate. If the humidity is very high, it will decrease slightly when the fan is on. If there is a freezer compartment, you need to make sure water does not drip from it onto what you are curing. On the warmest setting, the freezer unit doesn't freeze at all, so water collects in the drip tray; this needs to be cleared regularly.

If necessary, the humidity can be increased by leaving a bowl of heavily salted water (3:1 water to salt) on the bottom shelf. With the aid of a thermo-hygrometer (see p. 54) mounted on the inside of the fridge, and the occasional testing of acidity with a pH meter, you can create home-cured products of the highest standard in a domestic fridge. You just won't be the talk of the village for having bits of meat hanging around the place.

Dry curing ratios

Depending on the product, the ratio of salt to meat may or may not be critical.

- Whole muscles such as tenderloins and *coppa* are not reliant on precise curing ratios of salt to weight of meat. You could apply a 2 percent salt to weight of meat cure, but I tend to make an approximate cure in a tray with all the relevant ingredients mixed in and then just coat the meat on all sides. This dredging effect ensures that the surface area of the whole muscle is covered, which will be sufficient to cure it successfully. The length of time the meat is left in the cure depends on what you intend to do with it. For example, a tenderloin would need to be in the cure for only an hour if you were going to hot smoke it (see p. 218). However, if you were intending to turn it into an air-dried *filletto* (see variation, p. 178), you would need to leave it in the cure for a minimum of 1 day per 2.2 pounds (1 kg). This is also true of *coppa* (pp. 152–53).

- **Pancetta** requires a bit more thought because it is a dry cure that is applied once and allowed to turn into a brine. This cure is a precise 5 percent salt to weight of meat and the curing time is 3 days for every 1.1 pounds (500 g). After the allotted time, pancetta is traditionally rolled, tied, and air-dried, although you could cook with it right away. If you want to dry the pancetta and possibly eat it raw once it has lost around 30 percent of its original weight, it is important to make sure that the surface of the pancetta that becomes the internal rolled section has had sufficient contact with the cure, as it will now be in a mostly anaerobic condition.

- **Bacon** can be cured without the need to weigh out any ingredients; it can all be done by eye. If you have roughly equal amounts of sugar and salt, you will make a successful bacon cure. Additional ingredients such as bay leaves, cracked black pepper, and juniper berries make a perfect cure. You don't even need to weigh the pork before adding the cure in approximate handfuls – it is all very relaxed. A belly of bacon will require 5 days of curing and 5 days' drying before it is ready to eat. Canadian bacon will require 10 days of each because it is thicker.

- **Prosciutto-style hams** are completely buried in salt for 3 days for every 2.2 pounds (1 kg) and air-dried.

Any dry-cured item that has lost 30 percent of its original weight can be eaten raw.

Fermentation

While dry curing is the action of salt on raw meat, fermentation is all about acidity. This form of curing most often refers to making salami. It involves deliberately keeping coarsely ground meat at warm room temperature for a specific amount of time in order to encourage the growth of certain bacteria. The meat is then stuffed into a casing and allowed to mature, unrefrigerated for all, or part, of its life.

Raw meat and warm temperatures are not usually a good combination because bacteria will begin to multiply, causing the meat to spoil. However, if you add salt to the meat first, at a carefully calculated percentage, it arrests the production of

Salami mix

harmful bacteria, promotes desirable bacteria, and creates a natural acidity within the meat. The high acidity is key: you are looking for a pH of 4.9 or lower. You should check the acidity with a pH meter or strips (see p. 54) within the first week and then at regular intervals over the next 6 to 8 weeks until it is ready. With the correct acidity, achieved by the right percentage of salt, white blooms will eventually appear on the outside of the salami to enhance and protect it. (I like to add a dash of red wine as well, to further raise acidity.) Fermentation also changes the texture of the meat, leaving it firm and full of flavor.

The minimum amount of salt required for fermentation is 2 percent of the weight of the meat. However, I often suggest a range of 2 to 3 percent because it is better to oversalt slightly, as the salt is critical for fermentation to work successfully. At 3 percent, the saltiness won't be overbearing.

At River Cottage, we usually fill our casings with our precisely salted meat mixture and then hang the salami in a warm environment overnight before moving them on to air-dry. However, you could put the meat mix in a warm environment overnight first, and then fill the casings afterward. The advantage of this is that you can measure the pH before putting the mix in the skins and then use the mix as a salami starter – much like a sourdough starter for bread. I choose the former method because it involves handling the mix while it is still chilled and therefore working within a more controlled temperature range.

Backslopping

This rather unfortunately named technique (sometimes also called back batching) is a way of using a good fermented culture from a salami mixture to inoculate a fresh batch of meat. It's rather like making a sourdough bread starter and using it to get a batch of dough rising. This method is slightly more advanced than the tried-and-tested one above, and it is most often employed by professional artisanal charcutiers and *salumieri* who are making salami on a continual basis.

The advantage of this method is that it pretty much ensures that the finished salami will be very close to the taste and texture of every other salami made by that producer because it will contain the same positive bacteria and flavors.

The process for backslopping is easy: grind your meat and add 2 to 3 percent salt to the weight of meat. Add all your other ingredients and mix thoroughly by hand so that they are evenly distributed throughout the meat. Place the meat in a food-grade tray or box, cover tightly with plastic wrap, and put in a warm environment, 77°F to 81°F, to get the bacteria working and begin fermentation. You could also cover the box with a plastic bag for supersafety, which will stop any light from turning the fat rancid. After a period of 12 hours or so in this warm place, you can move the mixture to a fridge. Keep it in the fridge for weeks without doing anything to it.

After 4 weeks, remove the plastic wrap and you will see that the surface of the meat has become discolored and grayish, but underneath it's vibrant and pink. It should also begin to smell of salami. Transfer the fermented mixture to a clean bowl and remix it by hand so that the gray surface and pink underneath are combined.

You can use the fermented mixture to stuff into casings and make salami, which may slightly accelerate the process by a week or so. Set aside a small portion of the fermented mix and use it to kick-start your next batch by adding it to the fresh meat, thereby continuing with the process. The reserved fermented mix can be kept in the fridge for another 2 weeks before it is used to inoculate your next fresh salami mix.

If you are at all concerned about fermentation and yet still keen to make salami, you should consider adding a commercial nitrate cure, that is, cure #2 (see p. 31), along with a bacteria starter. At River Cottage, we use neither but are reliant on measuring the acidity with our pH meter and hanging in the correct conditions.

Wet curing (brining)

Wet curing usually involves immersing meat in a brine, which has a preservative effect. It also tenderizes and enhances the flavor. However, you still have to cook anything that has been submerged in a brine, no matter how long it is left in there.

Brining has an elementary combination of water and salt as its basis. This saline solution can then be enhanced with herbs, spices, sweeteners, and other seasonings to give it as much flavor as you require and, as long as you follow some simple rules on ratios of salt to liquid, you can be as creative as you like. Even the water can be partially replaced with other liquids, such as beer, cider, or apple juice.

At River Cottage, we make different strengths of brine for different products because they don't all respond to the brine in the same way. For example, we would not use the same strength of brine for a chicken breast as a pork shoulder.

Despite it sounding like the opposite of dry curing, wet curing has a similar effect on meat and fish. There is, though, an additional, seemingly contradictory action that takes place. Salt is a dehydrator and draws out moisture if applied in a dry cure. However, if you mix it with water, it has the effect of making meat more moist and juicy when cooked (Boxing Day ham and Thanksgiving Day turkey are traditionally brined before cooking).

This moisture-enhancing effect is thought to be because salt acts on the protein structure of meat, causing the normally tight-fitting "sheaths" around the muscle filaments to relax. Liquid from the brine is then deposited into the space that has been created and is retained even after cooking. This action also accounts for the fact that meat that is placed in brine will increase in weight by around 10 percent

Pig's head in brine

Turkey in brine

Brines

It is perfectly acceptable just to use the same simple brine for all your curing (and I have included a basic all-purpose one here), but should you start to feel more adventurous, I'd urge you to consider experimenting with brines that are specifically tailored for different produce. I have two separate brines for red meat and poultry (see p. 112), and all the recipes in this book adhere to their salinity and brining times – with further ingredients added for flavor.

Brines are easy to make. You simply measure out the liquid and salt, put them into a large stockpot, and add all the other ingredients, then bring the brine up to the boiling point, making sure you stir continuously so that the salt (and any sugar) dissolves. You then remove the pot from the heat and allow the brine to cool before chilling it overnight in the fridge.

Do not add any meat, fish, or poultry to a brine before it is completely cold, or you will be creating a dangerous soup of partially cooked, raw, and cured items. It is important that whatever you place in a brine is completely submerged. Putting a bowl on top to push down the meat usually works well.

Once the meat or fish is in the brine, chill it. The fridge is really the best place for this – although I have successfully left brining items in a cold room before, and this may be necessary if you are curing a large piece that won't fit in the fridge.

Brine works more quickly than dry salt alone, and so brining times are shorter than dry curing times. Precisely how long you need to leave the meat or poultry in the brine depends on the size and thickness of what you're curing and the strength of the brine. For reference, I have indicated generally accepted curing times for each of the basic brines on p. 112. Obviously, the longer you leave something in a brine, the saltier it will become. Meat can reach a point where it has absorbed too much salt, which will then be released during cooking, so it's important to follow recipes closely and, when in doubt, err on the side of caution with brining times.

If you make too much brine, you can refrigerate the surplus until you're ready to use it. However, I recommend that you discard a brine once it has been used, since it will have been diluted and will contain impurities drawn out by the salt.

Measuring salinity

Wet curing recipes always take into account the saltiness – or salinity – of the brine, which must be appropriate for the product being cured. You can generally just follow the recipe, but if you're interested (or if you have a strong flavor preference for the saltiness of your brines), you can calculate the salinity before making the brine. I have included my recommended salt levels in the basic brines on p. 112.

The easiest way to measure salinity is to use a brine tester, usually referred to as a brinometer, hydrometer, or salinometer (see p. 52). Simply float the brinometer in the liquid and read off the number on the scale that is level with the surface of the liquid. A brinometer measures in "salometer degrees," the highest being 100° and the lowest 0°. (This is not to be confused with the *percentage* of salt to liquid; the brinometer is in reality measuring liquid density, which is an indicator of salinity.)

You can use a brinometer only if the brine consists of just liquid and dissolved salt. If there are other ingredients – such as pieces of meat already curing – then the reading will tell you the density of the liquid rather than indicate how salty it is.)

Another way of measuring the saltiness of a cure you are making is to do a straightforward calculation: divide the weight of the salt by the combined weight of the salt and liquid, then multiply by 100. This will give you the overall percentage of salt to liquid. I have given salt-to-liquid percentages in the basic brines below.

If you want to create a brine from scratch using your own choice of ingredients and you want to make sure that the salinity is appropriate, then a brine table may be useful. The table opposite gives the amounts of salt and liquid required for different strengths of brine. These quantities make about a quart of brine; you can increase them as needed. The table is very precise, but you don't need to be too exact with measurements. If your brine is a little unsalty, it will just take longer to work. You will, of course, be cooking anything that has been wet cured, so there no health risk.

Basic all-purpose brine
For a simple brine, dissolve 300 g salt in 4540 ml water. If you're interested, the strength of this brine can be calculated: 300 ÷ (4540 + 300) x 100 = 6.1 percent salt to liquid. This percentage is equivalent to 23° on the brinometer scale. (See above for a fuller explanation.)

In order to make up the right volume of brine, you will generally need about half the amount of brine to the weight of meat.

Brine for red meat and pork
The brine I use for meat is quite strong, 20 percent salt to liquid, which is equivalent to about 80° salinity. I often use it for shoulders or legs of pork, and I like to add dark brown sugar as well as cider and apple juice (see Cider-cured ham, p. 195; Salt beef, p. 200; Brined Christmas turkey, p. 205). At River Cottage, we wet cure pork for 3 days per 2.2 pounds (1 kg), and beef, lamb, venison, or goat for no more than 1 day per 2.2 pounds (1 kg). The longer time for pork reflects the amount of fat it carries

Brine for poultry
This brine is subtler than the one used for meat. It has 10 percent salt to liquid, which is the equivalent to about 38° salinity. Poultry tends to dry out during cooking, and this brine is particularly good at keeping the breast meat moist. improves the flavor, too.

A whole turkey can be cured for 48 hours, while turkey breast is generally ready after 12 hours. A whole chicken or duck has an 8-hour cure in a wet brine, but the breasts require only 2 hours. You could possibly exceed these times by an hour or two for a particularly moist and tender result, though, of course, the meat will taste saltier, too.

Brining fish

In some parts of the world, fish is brined. A highly salty brine is used because of the high percentage of water in fish and the brining time is short – just an hour or two. In reality I don't think it is worth brining fish, so I haven't included a recipe.

BRINE TABLE

SALT (g)	LIQUID (ml)	PERCENTAGE OF SALT TO LIQUID (percent)
26.8	990	2.64
37.9	986	3.7
49	983	4.75
60.3	979	5.81
71.9	976	6.86
83.6	972	7.92
95.4	968	8.97
107.5	964	10.03
119.6	960	11.09
132	955	12.14
144.5	951	13.2
157.2	946	14.25
170.1	941	15.31
183.2	936	16.37
196.5	932	17.42
210	926	18.48
223.5	921	19.53
237.4	916	20.59
251.5	911	21.64

Smoking

I have a fairly rudimentary approach to smoking. That is not to say that I hold [it]
in anything other than the highest regard; I just prefer the simpler methods. Yo[u]
already know my views on equipment, so it will not surprise you to learn that bot[h]
my hot and cold smokers are cobbled together from recycled bits and bobs. On[e]
thing that is worth bearing in mind, though, is that smoke will inevitably b[e]
involved, so you should make sure that there is good ventilation or an exhaust fa[n]
in the place where you will be smoking.

Marked by a make-do-and-mend attitude inherited from my parents, I've mad[e]
my hot smoker from an old enamel bread box, and my cold smoker is an empt[y]
cider barrel connected to a garden incinerator via a length of vent ducting. The[se]
contraptions are unique and full of character, but, more important, they do the jo[b]
really well. If you want to replicate something similar yourself, see pp. 121–26.

Of course there are some amazing commercial, all-singing, all-dancing smoke[rs.]
I have seen high-end versions that look as if they could get you to Mars and bac[k.]
You could also have a hybrid homemade-commercial smoker. Hugh has [a]
commercial Maze firebox, which looks like a maze, in which he places wood chi[ps]
or sawdust. It sits in the bottom of his smoking chamber formed from an old gu[n]
cabinet. This is tall enough to allow the smoke to cool before wafting over t[he]
products hanging in there. There is more control and precision with a commerci[al]
smoker, but you'd be hard-pressed to say that they make things taste any bett[er.]
And the principles are the same, whether you use a commercial smoker or not.

There are two distinct forms of smoking, hot and cold. Hot smoking bo[th]
flavors and cooks. It is hot because the source of the heat is close to the produ[ct]
being smoked. The temperature you would hope to reach during the process[is]
between 122°F and 194°F. Anything more than that tends to dry things out to[o]
much. On occasion, if you are hot smoking and the internal temperature of t[he]
item you are smoking means it is not fully cooked, you might finish it off in a pa[n.]
I sometimes do this with large pork tenderloins.

Cold smoking flavors and preserves but does not cook. The item being smok[ed]
is separated from the heat source so that the smoke is cool by the time it reaches[.]
The ideal maximum temperature for cold smoking is 86°F. You will always need [to]
cook cold smoked meat, fish, or poultry before eating it (with the exception [of]
smoked salmon or trout).

Smoking cannot happen successfully unless the meat or fish has previously be[en]
cured with dry salt or in a brine. This is particularly important for any product th[at]
will be cold smoked and not cooked thereafter. Even in the case of hot smoki[ng,]
a cure must be applied first. The exceptions are cheeses or vegetables, which need[not]
be salted first.

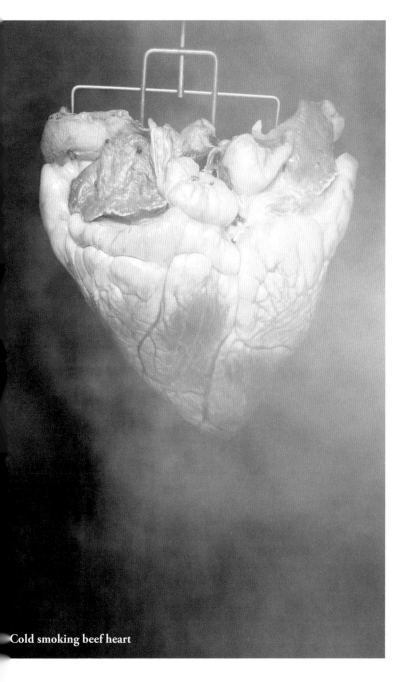

Cold smoking beef heart

It's important that anything to be smoked is washed under cold water after being salted, to make sure any residual cure and impurities drawn from the meat are removed. But it's critical that the item is then dried again. It should be thoroughly blotted with a clean cotton cloth or paper towels. This creates a slightly sticky surface, called a pellicle, and that is where the smoky flavor resides. It is a misconception that smoke penetrates a product. It does not. All the smoky flavors are deposited on the outer surface. If you smoke a product that is still wet, the smoke particles will attach themselves to the residual moisture on the surface and create a brown, slightly smoky sludge, which then rubs off.

Cheese, garlic, and certain vegetables don't form quite such a good pellicle as fish and meat. This means that though they are certainly worth smoking, you shouldn't expect them to develop the same depth of flavor as a side of bacon or a fillet of pollack. However, brined or lightly boiled vegetables that are allowed to cool and dry can take on an intense smoky tang (see Smoked new potato salad, p. 244).

Wood and smoke

I am obsessed with mixing woody cocktails from hardwood planks, chips, chunks, sawdust, and papers to get the perfect smoky flavor. There are endless combinations that all have their own characteristic flavor spectrum.

Most wood-smoke flavors are created when lignin, a compound found in all trees, is ignited and forms phenolic chemicals. Softwoods such as pine also contain toxic resins that create harsh and acrid notes in smoke. This is why you should only use hardwoods, such as oak, beech, or apple, for smoking food. You can, however, use pine needles for smoking, as these do not release harmful vapors.

Although you can create smoke from logs, twigs, or chippings left over from sawing, I recommend using fine sawdust, small shavings, or wood chips. The smaller pieces tend to burn evenly and consistently, giving a continuous flow of smoke, without forming flames. (If your fuel actually catches fire, you'll be topping up your firebox every 5 minutes, which is tedious, especially if you are cold smoking a large bacon loin that could take up to 12 hours.)

There are exceptions to the sawdust rule. When I smoke on a grill, which is a less precise art, I sometimes go for larger pieces of wood. And, should you be lucky enough to have a large inglenook fireplace, you can smoke foods suspended in the chimney above smoldering logs.

You can also buy wood "papers." Designed for the grill, these are thin pieces of wood that you soak in water then wrap around the item you are smoking. To my mind, they don't really deliver on flavor.

Another grill smoking method is to make use of a plank, which is also soaked and then placed directly on the charcoal. It is suitable for small items like burgers, steaks, and chicken and duck breasts. I have also used it for cheese (see p. 22

Commercial hot smoker

The smoky flavor is light, but the method does work well. It's a good way to introduce some subtle smokiness into your food before embarking on the full-blown home-smoking methods.

In addition to wood, I have used hay, pine needles, bay, lavender, rosemary, nettles, and juniper branches to create a more aromatic smoke at the end of a cold-smoking session, or for a blast of flavor during a quick hot smoke of something to be finished off in a pan or grill. I also like to use tea leaves in some recipes, such as my Cedar-smoked duck breasts on p. 226.

One of the great things about smoking is that somebody else's waste can be your fuel. At River Cottage, we have a constant supply of clean hardwood chips and sawdust from the local sawmill and various craftsmen and carpenters. If you are able to get hold of your fuel from a similar source, just make sure it is clean. For example, anything that has been cut down using a chainsaw may harbor residual traces of chain oil that would create a toxic smoke.

And if you're not fortunate enough to have a local supply, you can use the Internet to find wood chips and sawdust designed specifically for smoking.

The table below has an overview of wood types, smoke characteristics, and foods they complement well. But don't be limited by my suggestions. Create your own combinations and match them to anything you please.

WOOD TYPE	SMOKY CHARACTERISTICS	GOOD PAIRED WITH
Alder	Mild and delicate	Fish and poultry
Apple	Mild and fruity	Hams, game birds, and cheese
Cherry	Mild, sweet, and fruity	Duck and venison
Beech and ash	Moderate and exotic	Pork, fish, poultry, lamb, cheese, and vegetables
Oak	Strong, rich, and pungent	Beef, pork, and venison
Hickory	Strong, robust, and bitter	Beef

Hot smokers

Portable hot smokers are available in all shapes and sizes, and many of them come with a little spirit (alcohol) burner to place under the base and heat the sawdust to the smoldering point. However, they are of variable quality, so take a good look around and choose one that is robust and of simple design or, better still, make your own.

Mackerel fillets ready for hot smoking

Homemade hot smoker

Building a hot smoker

Together with other members of the River Cottage team, including Hugh and head chef Gill Meller, I have built and used several hot and cold smokers, both at our first HQ and now at our permanent home at Park Farm. We continue with the same basic designs first and foremost because they work really well. They are also easy to make and, yes, they have a certain rustic character that seems fitting for River Cottage.

Making a hot smoker is *so* easy that frankly the term *building* is a little flattering. It can take no more than 10 minutes and may not require any more skill than scavenging a few bits from around the house. If you can lay your hands on a suitable tin – a deep one with a snug-fitting lid, such as a cookie tin – improvise some kind of rack to fit inside it and locate a small pile of wood chips or sawdust; then, all you need is a heat source to plunk the tin on and you're ready to hot smoke.

Our own beloved hot smoker, formerly a bread box, fits the bill admirably. This photograph was taken the first time we put it together and used it. That was a while ago, and we've used it dozens of times since, with great success. A little heavier and bigger than a cookie tin, and with a lid that's easy to lift, it's still eminently portable and perfect for the job. We reckon it's still good for a few more years of heavy use.

To turn a metal bread box into a hot smoker, all you need to do is drill a couple of holes in each side, equally spaced and at the same height. Use an electric drill with a bit suitable for drilling metal. These holes can then support two close-fitting iron rods or metal grill skewers, which in turn support a rack. Make sure the length of the skewers or rods exceeds the width of the box by a couple of inches so they don't fall out. The rack needs to fit snugly inside. You can make a custom-size rack from chicken wire.

A ⅜-inch layer of wood chips or sawdust goes over the base of the smoker. This will be sufficient to smoke most things small enough to fit in this kind of smoker. The rack goes in with the food already on it (always first lightly salted, rinsed, and patted dry; see pp. 114–16), then the lid goes on. The box is then placed on the heat source – a gas burner, grill, or the smoldering coals of a beach or riverside fire. The base of the box heats up and the wood chips begins to smolder, making smoke. The inside of the box heats up, too – not to a very predictable temperature, given that the heat source varies, but with a bit of luck it will reach over 122°F and not exceed 194°F.

Depending on this temperature, and the thickness of the items being smoked, it may take anywhere from 15 minutes to 1 hour to complete the job and cook the food through. If the wood chips burn out before the food is cooked, you can add some more. To do this, you will have to remove the rack and food – with suitably protected hands – and start again.

If you don't trust your own DIY skills, or your old enamelware bread box is too precious to let go, you can, of course, buy a portable hot smoker. If it can be used over various heat sources, such as fires and gas burners, so much the better. Of course, if you are going to hot smoke on a gas stove top in your kitchen, you should make sure there is adequate ventilation – at best a good exhaust fan.

Cold smoking over an open fire

Before you launch into constructing a cold smoker, it's worth remembering that for centuries cold smoking was achieved by simply hanging meat and fish above an open fire, indoors or out. And it can still be done like that if you have the right kind of fireplace. In the seventeenth-century farmhouse at River Cottage HQ, we have an ideal inglenook fireplace, large enough to walk into and stand upright. We've fixed a metal bar across the chimney at a height where we can just stretch up and hang hams, fish, salami, and game. This is high enough that the smoke has time to cool before it reaches the food.

Ideally, for this sort of operation, you need low, smoldering embers. We would not hang anything in the chimney if the fire was hot enough to actually warm up the kitchen – the smoke would be too hot. Instead, we wait for the fire to die down and then hang product overnight. If the fire is still a bit too lively, we dampen it with wood chips that have been soaked in water.

The best way to test the temperature in the smoking zone is with a digital thermometer. However, you can also hold your hand above the fire, exactly where the product is going to hang. Ideally it should feel pleasantly warm (77°F to 86°F). You can just about get away with uncomfortably warm (95°F to 113°F), but any hotter than that and your meat or fish will get too dry – or even cook.

Building a cold smoker

If an existing fireplace is not an option, then the fulfilment of your cold smoking ambitions may require the construction, or at least customization, of a special bit of equipment. A cold smoker is larger, more complex, and definitely a bit more of a project than a hot smoker. Nevertheless, it's not difficult, and you will be rewarded for your efforts with wonderful cold smoked products.

Homemade cold smokers can take many forms but perhaps the simplest option is a version of the "three-piece" cold smoker we now use at River Cottage. There are three basic components:

- a firebox to generate the smoke
- some tubing, piping, or ducting to move and cool the smoke
- a smoke chamber to hold the smoke and the food being smoked

A cold smoker can either be custom-built or adapted from salvaged items, so a good rummage around a garage sale or a junk shop is a wise first move.

Homemade cold smoker

The firebox/smoke generator This is where the smoke is created, by burning wood chips or sawdust. At River Cottage, we have a firebox made out of an old bottled-gas cylinder. At home I use a galvanized metal garden incinerator. These are so good as fireboxes for cold smokers that they might as well have been designed specifically for that purpose. They are easy and cheap to buy, fare pretty well outside year-round, have neat, ready-made air holes to allow just enough oxygen flow to make wood chips smolder, and conical lids that fit perfectly onto a piece of vent ducting. Also, because of the material they are made from, they have a nice cool interior.

The only minor adjustment you have to make is to create a column of chicken wire mesh to go inside the box (about 6 inches in diameter and around 24 inches high), in which to place your fuel. A column of sawdust this high and wide will burn gently for 8 to 10 hours. To start the fire, you just need to put a couple of hot coal embers or some lit newspaper on the top of the sawdust column.

Alternatively, you could dispense with the firebox and position a commercial smoke generator, just as Hugh has, directly in the bottom of your smoke chamber – providing it is tall enough to allow the smoke to cool before it reaches the food above. This also takes away the need to incorporate tubing or piping.

The tubing/piping/ducting You'll need some kind of heatproof tubing that leads the smoke away from the firebox and over to the smoke chamber, allowing the smoke to cool as it does so. Spare bits of galvanized drainpipe (not plastic ones) will do the job but are rigid and hard to work with. Flue ducting is an obvious and more practical alternative, as it's actually designed for the job of moving smoke from one place to another. It's also flexible, so it can be adapted to the space you're working in, and is cheap enough to be bought and cut to the length you require. It should be at least a yard long – more if your firebox has a tendency to burn hot – to allow the smoke to cool as it travels to the smoke chamber.

The smoke chamber This is the space where the cooled smoke is contained, making contact with the food as it swirls lazily around. A few leaky spots are ideal, as totally airtight chamber won't draw properly. In some cases, a little chimney, at least a small hole in the top of the chamber, may be necessary to help the draw. A colander placed where the tubing or piping enters the smoke chamber at the bottom will dissipate the smoke, stopping it from becoming too much of a plume.

Our first smoke chamber was an old cider barrel, but the current one is made from recycled wood built into a large cabinet. The fish or meat is hung on loops of string from bars that run across the top of the wooden cabinet, though we can also insert racks, supported by some more bars across the middle of the cabinet, for smoking small fish or salami.

Other potential smoke chambers include old filing cabinets (the drawers can be adapted to hold racks and hanging bars), fridges, wooden wardrobes (beware of toxic paint, though), large metal garbage cans, old tea chests, or small sheds. You could even make a sturdy wooden box from scratch – anything from the size of a tea chest to a small walk-in wardrobe will work, depending on the extent of your ambition.

With any kind of smoke chamber, the ideal finishing touch is a temperature gauge set in the wall or door. Alternatively, you can measure the temperature from time to time using a probe thermometer, placed inside the chamber for 10 minutes while smoking. You should always try to keep the smoke chamber as cool as possible without letting the fire go out. Most of the time you should be in the desired 77°F to 86°F zone, but it can head north of 95°F in there on a very hot day, or when the firebox flares up a bit.

The temperature can be adjusted by altering the airflow through the smoker, which affects the intensity of the burn in the firebox. This can be done by covering or uncovering the air holes in the firebox, or by covering or uncovering the chimney on the smoke chamber. Either adjustment will make a difference of a few degrees.

Smoke shack If you have the space and the inclination to do quite a bit of smoking, a small walk-in smoke shack might suit you very well. In some respects, it is even simpler than the three-piece – being a one-piece, if you like. Effectively, it is a giant version of the hot smoker, in that sawdust is burned inside a sealed chamber, generating enough smoke to fill the whole space. Because of the sheer size of the chamber, the interior never gets too hot.

The classic customized smoke shack is an old wooden shed. Bars and racks for hanging and laying food on can be arranged at about head height. A steel plate or solid roasting pan is propped up on bricks on the floor. That may sound like madness, but provided you only ever light a small pile of sawdust in the center of the floor space (and it must have a concrete or earth floor, not a wooden one), you'll be okay. Under the bricks, and under the pan, goes a single gas burner (attached by rubber tubing to a portable gas bottle kept outside the shack). A pile of sawdust goes in the pan. The gas burner is lit and kept very low. The pile of sawdust is lit, too; the door is closed, and the smoking begins. The gas burner may be turned off once a good smolder is under way, and the sawdust can be relit or topped up, as necessary. A small vent or chimney hole may be needed to keep the smolder going, but as often as not, a less than airtight doorframe does the job on its own. If the shed isn't too big, you could also use a commercial firebox to create smoke.

This arrangement can be adapted for all sorts of confined spaces, provided they are fireproof. Of course, you should never attempt to do any kind of cold smoking inside a house, unless you can take advantage of a large chimney space above an open fire.

Fire and smoke management Remember, the whole point of cold smoking is to get the most possible smoke with the least possible heat – and fuel. In most cases, with the exception of open-fire smoking, a smoldering pile of sawdust is the best option. You'll need a few good handfuls of sawdust – more than you would use for hot smoking. A pile the size of a 2-pound (1 kg) bag of sugar should last 5 hours or more.

Lighting a pile of sawdust isn't always easy, and keeping it smoldering steadily can be tricky, too. The first tip is to keep your sawdust scrupulously dry; store it in a sealed plastic bag or a garabage can with a lid. The second is that a blowtorch is an extremely useful item for getting reluctant sawdust to start burning. Aerating the sawdust and lighting it from within helps, too, and a favored item with many cold smokers is a short piece of steel pipe with holes drilled in it, inserted into the bottom of the pile of sawdust. Stick the flame of your blowtorch in that and you'll soon be on your way. A chicken-wire column (see p. 124) is just as effective.

In all cases, except smoking over an open fire (where logs are recommended), you should burn your sawdust, once it's lit, with restricted ventilation. This is essential if the sawdust is to smolder, not flare up. But if you shut out the air entirely, the fire will soon extinguish itself. Successful management of a burn, and hence of a cold smoking session, is therefore more often than not down to the control of ventilation.

Opening the door of the firebox less than an inch (or the vent, if you have given it one) should increase the vigor of the burn. A small hole or little chimney in the top of the smoke chamber (if it doesn't leak already) will help draw the smoke through. Once the chamber is full of smoke, you can block it off – leaving perhaps just a tiny chink of a hole – with a smooth stone or block of wood. It's hard to be more specific than that, given that every home-built cold smoker will be different. But a decent bit of equipment put together in line with the ideas above should be fairly forgiving. A tweak here and a tweak there will see you right.

Damp and humidity One of the factors that most affects the success of your cold smoking is humidity – and this is obviously largely dependent on the weather. You need your smoke, and your smoke chamber, to be as dry as possible.

Commercial smokehouses recommend 20 percent humidity (not to be confused with the perfect air-drying humidity level of 60 to 80 percent). Commercial smokers often have some kind of dehumidifier built in to maintain conditions close to this level. At River Cottage we don't, and we don't worry about it either.

Cold smoking can be done pretty much year-round, but I would not attempt it on blistering summer days – which will increase the internal temperature of the smoke chamber – or damp, foggy, or rainy days, when the results are just not as good. There's no question that wetness is the enemy of a good smoke. For the same reason, any food you put in the smoker must itself be dry.

Cold smoked bacon

Grill smoking

Perhaps the gentlest way of beginning your smoking adventure is with a grill. A simple hot smoker, such as the one described on p. 121, sits very happily directly on the embers of a standard family grill, which is all you need to make the wood chips smolder into life.

However, with a slight upgrade to a kettle grill – basically a round grill base with a domed lid – you can cook and smoke a whole range of produce, such as pork tenderloin, mussels, oysters, fish fillets, duck breasts, and spiced butterflied leg of lamb (see pp. 218–29).

Cooking with fire

There is no great mystery to cooking with fire. It is one of the most basic methods of creating something edible from a raw state. I think that the primeval urge to make fire resonates with us all, but a few simple rules should be followed in order to move the results away from Paleolithic and toward culinary.

Forget trying to make do with a disposable version from the local garage – they are cheap, inefficient, and probably toxic. The smoke generated from the cheapest versions will be black and sooty and this will be transferred to anything you cook on them. You have no control with this kind of grill, and they burn quickly over a short period.

To get the best results when cooking and smoking with a grill, choose a charcoal-fired model, and one that has a lid. In order to successfully smoke as well as cook, it should have both top and bottom vents, which will allow you to control airflow and direct both smoke and heat. A kettle grill is relatively inexpensive and, with a small amount of effort – spent tending to the coals and wood chips to maintain temperature and smoke – should serve you well. (A foil pan or stainless steel bowl filled with water, placed on the cooking rack next to the food, can further moderate temperature.)

If you would prefer something a bit more upmarket that requires less manual input to control temperature (and that can hold temperatures over a longer period, particularly in the lower temperature range), you should probably opt for a water smoker.

Water smokers look like elongated kettle grills divided into three sections. The fuel section is on the bottom and contains a vent for airflow control. There is a middle section that holds a water pan that acts as a buffer between the heat of the fuel and the food on the grill above. The top section will have a lid with a thermometer and also contain a vent.

Because the heat reaches the food indirectly, the cooking is more in the form of convection or roasting than grilling. The separation of the food from the fuel by the water pan means the cooking temperature can be controlled easily and has ange between 175°F and 465°F. This is particularly useful for cooking and smoking large items over a long period, such as a whole leg of lamb. Even though this form of cooking is at relatively low temperatures, it is still hot smoking. Cold smoking really needs to take place below 86°F, and no grill, not even a water smoker, can achieve that.

I like to use pure hardwood charcoal for grilling – made from hardwood logs that have been heated to a high temperature in a low-oxygen environment. This stops the logs from burning too much but dries out all the sap and moisture, leaving a carbonized lump. This sort of charcoal is easy to light and burns evenly over a long time, producing gentle white smoke.

You can buy hardwood briquettes, which are compressed lumps of pure hardwood charcoal, but do not confuse these with standard barbecue briquettes, which are often made from coal and such materials as clay and limestone held together with cornstarch and coated in lighter fluid that will flavor your food adversely. Make sure any charcoal you buy is from a sustainable source.

How to smoke on a charcoal grill

Most kettle grills have either a grate or a basket for the charcoal. If you want to hot smoke anything for a period of 30 minutes or longer, position the charcoal so that it covers only one side of the grate. This leaves room on the other side to place an aluminum foil pan that can be filled with water if you want to try to lower the cooking temperature. There is no need to use water if you just want a quick cook and smoke. Instead of a foil water pan, you could dampen the wood chips briefly before applying.

Pile the charcoal so that it is two or three lumps deep and light it. If you are going to cook for longer than 30 minutes, you should place the foil pan of water in position, filled to the three-quarter mark. Open the bottom vents completely and place the cooking grill in position over the charcoal (and water). Some grills have hinges that allow you to add more charcoal and, equally important, wood, without having to dismantle the whole grill. Place the lid on top and completely open the top vent to create a good draw of air.

After 10 minutes, the coals will be turning gray and the necessary temperature will be reached. At this point, add the wood chips to the burning charcoal and replace the lid.

When smoke starts to pour through the top vent, open the lid and place your food on the grill directly above the foil pan of water (if cooking for more than 30 minutes). Replace the lid. I like to position the top vent on the opposite side to the lit charcoal so that the smoke is drawn over the food before leaving via the vent. You can control the smokiness through the amount of wood added to the lit charcoal and also by closing the vent so that the smoke envelops the food for longer.

Kettle grill

How to smoke on a water smoker

With the middle and top sections of the grill removed, place a layer of charcoal on top of the grate, within the ring, and light it with the vents open. When the charcoal starts to develop a gray dusting of ash, place the middle section, with an empty water basin suspended in it, over the charcoal. The middle section has an access door so that you can add more coals or wood and this should be closed.

Fill the water pan three-quarters full with water as soon as the middle section is in position. Put the cooking grills in place one on top of the other and put the lid on top. Leave the top vent completely open, but adjust the bottom vent so that it is only half open. This will allow the grill to reach its ideal cooking range. When the thermometer is in the correct range (i.e., 194°F to 230°F), you can open the access door and put the wood chips on the charcoal.

When the smoke pours through the top vent, it is time to place the food on the cooking grills and replace the lid. The temperature might initially drop a little but should crawl back up after 10 minutes or so. You can further control the temperature by opening up the bottom vents to increase the heat and closing the top vent if the temperature is too high. The charcoal should easily burn for 4 hours in a water smoker, although the water will need to be replaced every 2 hours. The water pan can also be accessed via the door in the middle section.

Grill rubs and marinades

Although I think it's important to treat your main ingredient with respect and never to mask or overpower it, grilling does provide ample opportunity to experiment with rubs and marinades, creating robust flavors and toothsome, sticky textures that enhance the meat or fish you are cooking.

Rubs

When you are smoking on a grill, you will need to apply salt to the item you are cooking too – not in the same quantities as if you were actually curing it, but enough to create the sticky pellicle (see p. 116). This salt can often be part of a flavorsome rub.

Rubs are mostly a combination of ground spices, herbs, and other aromatics and seasonings, including sugar and salt. They should be gently massaged all over the item that you intend to hot smoke and allowed to flavor it for at least 30 minutes before cooking.

Rub flavorings can be divided into roughly six categories: hot, sweet, herby, earthy, sharp, and salty. Hot and sweet work brilliantly together, and so do earthy and herby, while sharp flavors go well with anything on the grill. Try one of my suggestions or make up your own combination from the chart on page 132.

Steak rub This is an excellent way to pep up steaks. Using a pestle and mortar, coarsely grind 2 teaspoons each black peppercorns and yellow mustard seeds with 2 teaspoons paprika and 1 teaspoon each brown sugar and sea salt.

Hot and sweet rub This is ideal for red meat, pork, and poultry. In a small bowl, mix together 2 tablespoons each dark brown sugar and ground cinnamon, 2 teaspoons each dried thyme and sea salt, 1 teaspoon grated nutmeg, and ½ teaspoon each ground allspice and mace.

RUB FLAVORINGS

HOT	SWEET	EARTHY	HERBY	SHARP
Black pepper	Allspice	Caraway	Basil	Garlic
Cayenne	Cinnamon	Cumin	Bay	Mustard
Chile	Cloves	Paprika	Dill	Turmeric
	Nutmeg		Fennel	
	Honey		Marjoram	
	Maple syrup		Oregano	
	Sugar		Parsley	
			Rosemary	
			Sage	
			Thyme	

Marinades

These are a bit slower than rubs in their action. Often oil based and supplemented with herbs, spices, fruit, or chopped aromatics such as garlic and onion, they allow flavor to permeate into the main product, but they may also include an acid ingredient such as vinegar or citrus juice that helps to tenderize it.

Spread the marinade all over the meat or fish and allow at least an hour for it to work, but overnight in the fridge is preferable to reach maximum flavor. Start off using one of my favorite marinades that follow, then experiment with different combinations of acid, oil, and aromatics from the chart opposite.

Tikka marinade This is excellent for boneless lamb and poultry. In a small bowl mix together 2 tablespoons each garam masala, grated fresh ginger, and plain yogurt; 2 teaspoons each chile powder, ground fenugreek, and ground coriander; 1 teaspoon sea salt; 4 cloves garlic, chopped; good squeeze of lime juice; and 1–2 tablespoons sunflower oil.

Citrus marinade This works particularly well with fish and poultry. In a small bowl, whisk together ¼ cup extra-virgin olive oil, 2 tablespoons cider vinegar, ¼ cup chopped fresh tarragon, finely grated zest and juice of 1 orange and 1 lemon, a good pinch of sea salt, ½ teaspoon black pepper, and 2 cloves garlic, finely chopped.

Mustard marinade This works well with red meat, pork, poultry, and seafood. In a small bowl, whisk together 3 tablespoons each mustard (of choice), extra-virgin olive oil, and balsamic vinegar; a splash of Worcestershire sauce, 2 cloves garlic, finely chopped; 1 teaspoon chopped fresh thyme, and pinch of sea salt.

MARINADE FLAVORINGS

ACID	OIL	AROMATICS	
Cider	Canola	Allspice	Ginger
Citrus juice	Hemp	Black pepper	Onion
Soy	Olive	Chile	Oregano
Vinegar	Sesame	Coriander seeds	Paprika
Wine		Dill	Rosemary
		Garlic	Thyme

Tips for successful grill smoking

Get the grill prepared in advance – and don't let the beer and wine flow too freely before you fire it up. Alcohol, fire, smoke, and raw meat mingle happily but can be disastrous if combined in the wrong quantity or order.

Make sure the grill is clean from the previous use. There is no reason to get sloppy about hygiene and food safety just because you are out of the kitchen. Invest in a good wire brush to clean the cooking grills and make sure that soot and ash haven't blocked off any of the air vents.

Store your charcoal and wood chips in bins or containers so they remain dry and safe (and free of any unwanted ingredients contributed by next door's cat).

Put your grill on a flat surface, away from anything that might catch fire, and don't leave it unattended, particularly if there are young children present. If you haven't invited the neighbors over, make sure they have not just hung out their washing.

Once the grill cooking and smoking is completed, shut the vents, replace the lid, and allow the remaining fire to slowly die down to ash at low temperatures. Don't try to quickly cool a lit grill by pouring water on it, as this will just create a horrible sticky mess. And don't attempt to transport or move a grill that hasn't completely cooled down.

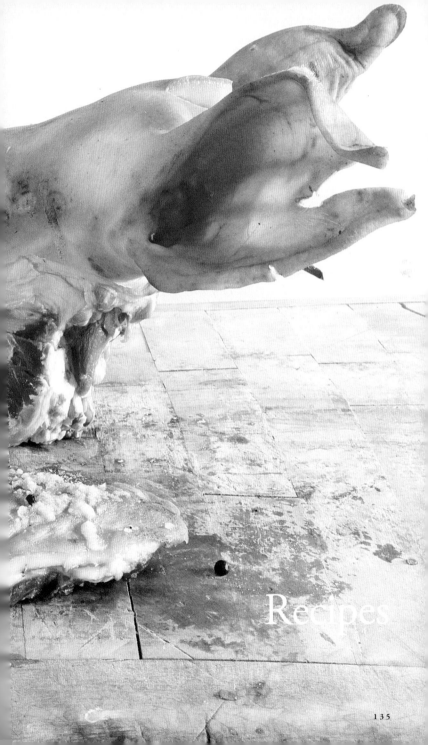

Recipes

These recipes are sound and tested, but there is flexibility in most of them, as long as the core method is adhered to. The aim is not to have you knocking out identical products, as if from a template. You should allow for, and embrace, some positive contingency. Quite apart from the ingredients themselves, slight differences in humidity, temperature, or the weather will lead to subtle change in the end result. Using different cuts of meat may even result in products you prefer. Take it all as part of the ongoing experience, and be happy in the knowledge that you are applying yourself to one of the oldest culinary frontiers.

The recipes are roughly arranged according to the method of curing involved, starting with the simplest techniques and progressing to more advanced methods. Although there are some recipes where the main ingredients are set (you wouldn't veer away from beef, for instance, if you wanted to make classic pastrami), I hope you will try all sorts of variations. I have included suggestions along the way.

Cured products such as confits, pâtés, hams, bacon, and salami rely on slightly different techniques, but they are connected by the use of salt and fat, and most, while requiring very few ingredients, become much more than the sum of their parts. Confits are usually cooked in fat, which seals and preserves the meat when the fat is cooled and hardened. Pâtés are also cooked but have a nice balance of fat and salt to give them a moist texture. Often at River Cottage we line the pâté mold or pan with bacon and use offcuts of cured bacon to add flavor.

Hams can be dry salted or immersed in a brine – either to be air-dried over many months then eaten raw or to be cooked in a pot like a Christmas ham. They take in a whole gamut of techniques, including dry curing, brining, and sweetening with sugar, syrup, or honey. Ham can be rolled like a pancetta with spices, then added to soups, stews, or pasta sauces, or simply sliced and eaten raw after cold smoking. Salami require casings and a specific fat and salt ratio that allow fermentation to happen. This method requires precision and some skill but is absolutely accessible to anyone willing to try.

Of course you should cook the recipes that most appeal to you, but there is one joint of meat I recommend you make part of your shopping list: the pork sirloin. This is inexpensive and incredibly versatile: it can be dry cured, brined, and hot and cold smoked. You can learn everything there is to know about curing, smoking, drying, molds, and bacteria by applying all the traditional methods to it. What's more, the relatively small size of a normal sirloin cut means it can be ready to eat in a short time. A dry cured sirloin, salted in the style of a prosciutto ham, is ready within 4 months, as opposed to at least a year for the traditional whole leg. Similarly, a brined and cold smoked sirloin, cooked in the same way as a cider cured ham, takes days instead of weeks to make it to the dinner table. There is no place for impatience in smoking and curing – we are not dealing with fast food here – but a sirloin cut takes the steepness out of a wonderful learning curve.

Dry cured bacon

TECHNIQUES	Dry curing, air-drying, cold smoking (optional)
CURING TIME	Minimum 10 days

The daily application of a simple cure, consisting of sugar, salt, and a few aromatics to a small, inexpensive piece of pork belly creates perfect bacon in just 10 days. You will learn almost everything you need to know about curing and hanging a piece of meat from this straightforward recipe, which is illustrated with step-by-step photographs on pp. 140–41. It is simple but effective: the charcuterie equivalent of a haiku.

Makes about 100 medium slices

4.4 lb (2 kg) free-range pork belly,
  in one piece, skin on, flat rib
  bones intact

For the cure
1.1 lb (500 g) PDV salt
2½ cups (1.1 lb/500 g) Demerara sugar
A few bay leaves, shredded
About 20 juniper berries, lightly bruised
3 tbsp (0.88 oz/25 g) black peppercorns,
  freshly ground

Equipment
Food-grade bowl
Food-grade box or tray
Meat slicer (optional)

If your pork belly carries an even covering of flare fat, keep it in place. An uneven covering of flare fat could affect the curing time, so it is better to remove it and render it to make lard. The fat is easy to remove: just pull it away by hand. It will keep in the freezer for months.

Place all the cure ingredients in a clean food-grade container. A rounded bowl is ideal because it enables you to thoroughly mix the ingredients with no pockets of salt, sugar, or flavorings caught in any corners.

Place a handful of this cure in the base of a food-grade box or tray big enough to hold the piece of belly. You might find the salad drawer in the bottom of your fridge is perfect for this. Add the piece of belly, skin side down, and scatter another handful of cure over the surface (pic 1, p. 140). You should use about one-fifth of the cure on this first day. Lightly rub the cure into the meat, making sure that the sides are also coated (pic 2, p. 140). You do not need to massage the cure hard into the pork belly but make sure it is evenly coated (pic 3, p. 140).

Slide the salad drawer back into the fridge or, if you are using a separate container, cover it with a clean tea towel and put it in the fridge or in a cool place such as a larder. Leave for 24 hours. In the meantime, store the cure in an airtight plastic container so it doesn't absorb moisture from the air and become damp.

The next day, there will be a pool of liquid in the container with the pork belly – a mixture of moisture drawn out from the meat and dissolved cure (pic 4, p. 140). This is the curing process in action. Lift out the belly (pic 5, p. 141) and pour off this liquid. There is no further culinary use for it. There is no need to be too fastidious, and it is fine if some residual traces of dissolved cure remain in the drawer.

Now put a fresh handful of the cure into the container and place the pork belly back on top. You can rotate the belly in order to even out the application of cure mix, but this isn't strictly necessary. As before, rub the belly with more cure mix – again, aim to use about one-fifth of what you started with.

Repeat this process for up to 5 days. You will notice that the belly will get firmer and darker in color and there will be less liquid to pour away each day as the meat cures and dries.

After 5 days of applying cure, take the belly out of the container and run it under cold water. Then clean the surface of the meat with a cloth soaked in malt vinegar and pat dry (pic 6, p. 141).

At this point, you can pop your meat back into the container (cleaning it out first) in the fridge or larder. Alternatively, assuming it's the right time of year, you can hang the meat outside (see p. 103). Insert hooks along one end of the belly or skewer onto a rack of hooks, often called a "bacon comb" (pic 7, p. 141). Find a spot out of direct sunlight where the air can get to the meat and hang the meat there (pic 8, p. 141) for 5 days. If you like, wrap the belly in cheesecloth, but this is not necessary.

You do not have to do anything to it during this period. However, you might want to give it a cursory check every now and then, particularly if you are hanging it outside. In the winter months, you will not have to worry about flies laying eggs on the meat, but it is good practice to check it regularly to see if the sun is on it at certain times of the day, or to see if there is a breeze blowing over it.

After 5 days, it will be ready to slice with a sharp knife or meat slicer and eat. It will be the best bacon you have ever had.

(recipe continues on p. 142)

Curing and hanging pork belly

Dry cured bacon, *continued*

You can keep the bacon hanging in a cool place, or store it in the fridge, for up to 3 months. It will become firmer the longer you leave it, and the flavor will intensify. Cut slices as you need them, removing the bones as you come to them. Slices can be kept in the freezer.

After 4 to 5 months of drying, the belly will become so firm that it will no longer be possible to slice it, but you can take chunks from it to add to soups, stews, or pasta sauces. Eventually, it will become very hard and you will be able to carve only shards from it, which can be eaten raw. However, it is unlikely that you will have the willpower to allow it to get to this stage!

If you want to smoke your bacon, allow it to dry for 10 to 14 days before you do so. This will ensure that it is fully cured and will not be susceptible to negative bacteria, which are sometimes present in a smoking environment. You can then place it in your cold smoker and smoke it for 8 to 10 hours.

Variation

Canadian bacon   If you want to make your own Canadian bacon, use a loin of pork. As this meat is thicker, you will need to apply the cure for 10 days and follow with 10 days' hanging and resting.

As with the belly, it is better to keep the loin on the bone. If you remove the bone at this stage, you will be left with "peaks and troughs" in the meat where the cure can collect and act unevenly.

There is a significant part of the spine in the loin, called the chine, which needs to be removed because it acts as a barrier to the cure. It extends the whole length of the loin and looks triangular. To remove it, you need to use a butcher's saw and cut along the spine at an angle, so as not to cut into the meat underneath the bone. It's quite a tricky operation but perfectly possible to do yourself (see p. 68). Alternatively, your butcher should be happy to do it for you. The main issue is that the saw needs to cut horizontally, and toward your other hand. With care, the chine bone will come away, leaving a line of exposed rib ends underneath. These are often called buttons because of their circularity.

Once the initial drying time of 10 days has passed and you want to take a few slices off your cured bacon, remove the bones as necessary. A quick and effective way of removing them is to get a looped piece of butcher's string, or even a cheese wire, around the "button" part of the ribs and then pull down along the bone. With a bit of effort, the rib will come away from the bacon, stripped of all the meat and sitting proud. It is then a simple operation to release it at the other end. These bones can be added to stocks to deepen the flavor.

Rolled pancetta

TECHNIQUES	Dry curing–brine hybrid, air-drying
CURING TIME	Minimum 12 days

Traditionally, a pancetta is a boned and rolled cured piece of pork belly that, depending on its age, is either cooked and used for dishes such as spaghetti carbonara or eaten raw. This is really a more advanced version of the bacon on pp. 138–42. The difference here is that the skin and bones are removed and the meat is rolled and tied. Also, with pancetta, the liquid is not removed as the belly cures but allowed to create a brine that envelops the belly. In essence, you are making a dry cure that turns into a wet cure.

The cure itself requires precise measurements because you make only one application. The golden rules are that the salt in your cure mix should be 5 percent of the starting trimmed, skinned, and boned weight of the pork belly – so 3.5 ounces (100 g) salt for a 4.4-pound (2 kg) piece of belly – and to allow 3 days of curing for each 1.1 pounds (500 g).

For ease, the recipe assumes you're using a normal-size cut, but if you are using a different-size piece of meat, you should calculate the salt accordingly.

Makes about 100 round slices

4 lb (2 kg) free-range pork belly, in one piece
1 clove garlic, crushed (optional)

For the cure

5 oz (100 g) PDV or other additive-free salt
2 tbsp (1.4 oz/40 g) black peppercorns, coarsely ground
2 tbsp (1.8 oz/50 g) packed dark brown sugar
2 tsp (0.35 oz/10 g) juniper berries, crushed

2 tsp (0.14 oz/4 g) coarsely grated nutmeg
4 sprigs thyme
4 bay leaves, shredded

Equipment

Vacuum or ziplock food bag
Vacuum-sealer machine (optional)
Butcher's string
Food-grade tray
Meat slicer (optional)

Using a sharp filleting knife, remove all the flat ribs from the belly (see p. 70); save for adding to stocks. It is also best to remove any flare fat (see p. 81), which you can freeze or render for roast potatoes, as for duck fat (see p. 207).

(continued)

Remove the uppermost part of the skin from the fat by cutting just under the rind and stroking the tip of the knife underneath until you can begin to peel it back in one piece. This skin has several uses, such as placing on top of a stew, which it will thicken, or barding (wrapping around) lean meat, such as venison or rabbit, to prevent it from drying during cooking. Trim the belly to make a neat square and, as ever, don't waste the trimmings; keep them for pasta sauces, soups, and stews.

Keeping back half of the black pepper, mix the ingredients for the cure together in a bowl. Put half the cure in a vacuum or ziplock food bag. Put the pork belly in the bag, laying it on top of the cure, and then spread the remaining cure on the uncovered side of the pork belly so that it is sandwiched between the cure.

Seal the bag and place in a shallow food-grade tray in the fridge. Allow 3 days of curing for each 1.1 pounds meat. Without removing it from the bag, massage the cure into the belly every now and again to redistribute all the ingredients evenly.

After the allotted curing time, remove the belly from the bag, wash off any residual cure under cold running water, and pat the meat dry with a clean tea towel. Lay the belly, fat side down, on a board and rub crushed garlic all over the inside of the meat. Sprinkle the reserved pepper onto the area just rubbed with garlic.

Position the pork belly so that the natural top part is away from you, and roll the bottom toward it; these will almost certainly be the two longest sides. Roll as tightly as you can. To keep it in place until you tie the first knot, you can use skewers. Your meat is now ready to tie using the butcher's knot (see pp. 148–49).

Once the pancetta is rolled and tied, it is ready to hang in a cool, humid place (see p. 103) out of direct sunlight – or you can place it on a tray in the fridge. The humidity stops the pancetta from drying out too quickly.

Traditionally, pancetta was created to cook with and not necessarily allowed to dry out completely. However, if nice and dry, it certainly works well on a charcuterie plate. You can start to cook with your pancetta right away, though you are slightly cheating yourself because it will have much more flavor if left to hang for 2 to 3 weeks.

The pancetta will be mature enough to eat raw after 4 to 6 weeks or, as a general rule, once it has lost around 30 percent of its original weight. It will last a couple months or longer in the fridge. Either slice with a sharp knife or meat slicer.

Variation

Lambcetta This works as well as pancetta in pasta sauces. Replace the pork belly with lamb's breast, another inexpensive cut. I always cook lambcetta (as I call it) rather than eat it raw because I find lamb fat more palatable this way.

Tying the butcher's knot

Always start with your first knot in the middle and then one at each end (this wi
stop the rolled joint from splaying out). Add knots between at 2-inch or so interval
For pancetta, the strings need to be supertight to ensure there are no pockets of ai
and to account for any shrinkage as the meat dries. For boned and rolled meat t
be cooked, the string needn't be tight – it simply needs to keep the joint in shape

To tie the butcher's knot, make a small knot at the end of the length of butcher
string (pic 1). Place the string underneath the rolled pancetta with the small knc
pointing away from you in the 12 o'clock position. Pick up the knotted end an
pass it over the pancetta and under and around the back of the tail part of strin
(pic 2); you will need to pass it from one hand to the other.

Loop the knotted end over the top of the string sitting on the pancetta and pa
the knot under and then up through that loop (pic 3), then pull until it forms
second knot below the original small knot. Let go of the small knotted end.

Pick up the long tail and pull this upward (pic 4) and toward you so that the tw
knots are forced together, causing the string around the pancetta to shorten ar
tighten (pic 5). Pull as hard as you can so that the string will not become baggy
the meat dries out and reduces in size. Cut the string close to the knots (pic 6).

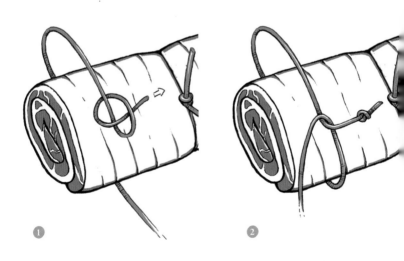

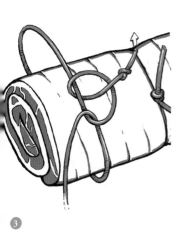

3

4

5

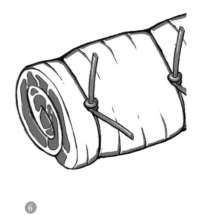

6

Lardo

TECHNIQUE	Dry curing
CURING TIME	Minimum 3 months

Lardo is pure cured pork fatback, a simple but exquisite food. The world's most famous *lardo* has been made in the hamlet of Colonnata, in northern Italy, for centuries. Here, Carrara marble is mined, a stone of such quality that Michelangelo's *David* was carved from it. The same highly prized marble is used to make casks in which *lardo* is cured, not only keeping it cool and blocking out light (which would turn it rancid) but also imbuing the fat with its own minerals, so that it takes on a subtle flavor unique to that place.

You can't, of course, re-create that special product, but you can make something similar, and very delicious. *Lardo* should be sliced gossamer-thin and can be eaten raw with a small amount of olive oil or, as I particularly recommend, wrapped around freshly steamed asparagus so that it becomes translucent and melting.

Makes about 1.1 lb (500 g)

A slab of thick pork fatback, skin on,
 about 2.2 lb (1 kg)

For the cure

8.8 oz (250 g) coarse sea salt
tsp (0.52 oz/15 g) black peppercorns,
 freshly cracked
tsp (0.7 oz/20 g) juniper berries, bruised

10 clove garlics, very finely chopped,
 almost to a paste
3 or 4 sprigs rosemary or thyme
0.17 oz (5 g) bay leaves, finely shredded

Equipment
Ziplock food bag

For the cure, put the salt, pepper, juniper berries, garlic, and herbs in a bowl and mix well. Put the pork fat in a ziplock food bag (in which it will fit snugly coated in the cure) and pour in the cure. Seal the bag.

Gently massage the cure around all the sides of the pork fat (the cure mix must be in constant contact with the surface of the fat). Put the ziplock bag into a black plastic bag to stop light from getting to it and refrigerate for 3 to 6 months. Although not typical, I place a weight on top, as it gives the lardo a pleasing density.

When the lardo is ready, remove the outer rind of skin in a single sheet (use this to add body to a soup or stew, placing it on top). Slice the lardo extremely thinly and serve. Lardo will keep, wrapped in black plastic, in the fridge indefinitely.

Coppa

TECHNIQUE	Dry curing
CURING TIME	Minimum 8 weeks, plus 2 days

Coppa is a classic Italian cured meat made from the "eye" of the muscle that extends from the shoulder of a pig into the neck. The piece of meat itself is also called the *coppa*, which roughly translates as "nape" (as in neck). At River Cottage we usually remove it from a sparerib joint before we grind the rest of the meat for sausages or salami. The *coppa* is pretty easy to remove – it's simply a case of seaming out (i.e., dividing) a set of muscles. Once located, it will practically show you where to make the cuts (see pp. 64 and 67). Alternatively, a good butcher will do this for you.

The curing method requires salt at 3 percent of the weight of the meat and 1 day's curing per 2.2 pounds (1 kg) of meat. Alternatively, you could apply the salt box method (see p. 98). The following recipe is based on an average uncured *coppa* weight of about 4.4 pounds (2 kg).

Makes 1 coppa (about 3 lb/1.4 kg)

1 free-range pork coppa (see above),
    about 4.4 lb (2 kg)
Beef bung casing (lower intestine)

For the cure

2.1 oz (60 g) PDV or other
    additive-free salt
3½ tsp (0.35 oz/10 g) white peppercorns,
    freshly ground
7 tsp (0.7 oz/20 g) black peppercorns,
    freshly cracked

1 tsp ground cinnamon
2 or 3 cloves, crushed
20 juniper berries, bruised
2 or 3 bay leaves, shredded
A glass of white wine

Equipment

Ziplock food bag
Food-grade tray
Butcher's string
Meat slicer (optional)

Put all of the ingredients for the cure in a bowl and mix thoroughly. Put the pork coppa into a ziplock food bag, pour in the cure, and seal the bag. Massage the cure into the meat so that it gets a liberal covering.

Put the bag on a tray and place in the fridge. Leave the coppa to cure in the fridge for the allotted time (1 day per 2.2 pounds/1 kg), giving it a gentle massage every other day. On the penultimate day, put the bung casing to soak in cold water.

Take the meat out of the bag and wash off the cure under a cold running tap. Wipe it dry. I like to wipe a clean cloth soaked in wine over the meat at this point because it gives a nice acidic, clean surface to the coppa, which will protect it.

Place the meat in the casing (just like putting on a sock). Secure both ends with string, then tie along the length of the coppa using the butcher's knot (see pp. 148–49). Prick with a sterilized pin so that any air bubbles will be released; this will allow the skin to shrink back with the meat during the drying-out process.

Put the coppa back in the fridge and leave to cure for 8 to 10 weeks, until it has lost 30 percent of its original weight. Try to maintain an average temperature of around 50°F or so (which should be possible in a domestic fridge).

When it is ready, the coppa will be firm to the touch with a little bit of give. Slice it thinly and remove the casing before eating. It is excellent served with thinly sliced beets.

Variations

There are several ways to customize your coppa using different ingredients. You can replace the cinnamon, cloves, juniper, and bay with spices such as cayenne and paprika, or try a mellow fennel seed version.

Gravlax with beets

TECHNIQUE	Dry curing–brine hybrid
CURING TIME	Minimum 3 days

This is a classic, adapted from *The River Cottage Fish Book*. The beets in the cure are my addition. The vegetable has no real curing properties, but it has plenty of flavor of course, and immense visual impact. Colored with the beets, the salmon is reminiscent of a sunset watched from a tropical island.

Serves 10 to 15

2 sides (large fillets) of wild salmon, about 2.2 lb (1 kg) in total

For the cure

½ cup (3.5 oz/100 g) superfine sugar
2.6 oz (75 g) PDV or other additive-free salt
5 tsp (0.52 oz/15 g) black or white peppercorns, or a mixture, coarsely ground

A large bunch of dill, coarse stalks removed, finely chopped
2 or 3 cooked beets, peeled and grated

Equipment

Kitchen tweezers
Food-grade tray

With tweezers remove the pin bones that run down the center of the fish fillets.

Mix all the ingredients for the cure together in a bowl. Place a good handful of the cure on the bottom of a food-grade tray. Lay the first salmon fillet, skin side down, on top, then cover with more cure. Top with the second fillet, skin side down, and cover again with cure. Put a board on top, weigh down, and place in the fridge.

Leave the fish to cure for at least 3 days (for smaller fillets) and up to 7 days (for really big fillets from an 11-pound [5 kg] or larger salmon). Every day, turn the "fillet sandwich" over and baste the fish in its accumulated juices, then replace the weight.

When the fish is cured, rinse the fillets and pat them dry. The outside of the fillet will be stained purple and will have a wonderful gradient of purple and orange along the thin slices. Serve with lightly buttered rye bread.

Note: Unsliced gravlax can be wrapped and kept in the fridge for up to 10 days.

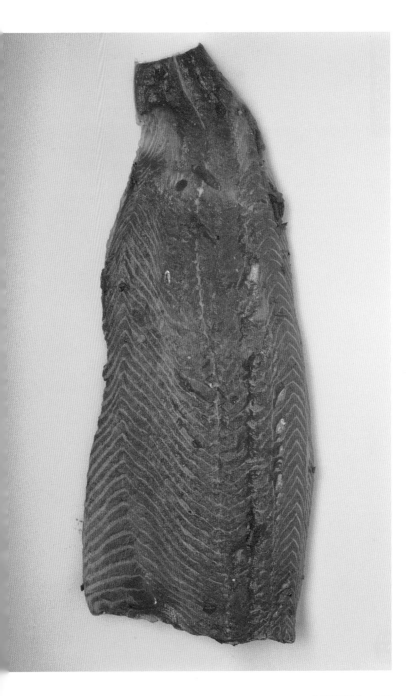

Prosciutto

TECHNIQUES	Total immersion method, air-drying
CURING TIME	Minimum 12 months

This is the start of a wonderful journey, one that will take you all the way back to the beginning of curing culture and involve over a year of your life. Of all the recipes I teach at River Cottage, this is the one that really convinces people that they can produce an authentic, traditional cured product, no matter where they live or how inexperienced they may be.

Dry curing and air-drying a leg of pork will test your nerve because it is such a long time before you get to the payoff. It will be a roller coaster of emotions, triggering the worries you'd expect when meat is unrefrigerated, covered in mold, and, from the outside, not appetizing in appearance. Let those doubts come and go. Follow these simple instructions; be vigilant, confident, and patient; and, in time, you will create one of the finest examples of cured meat there is.

Although this follows an authentic method, you shouldn't expect to produce something that tastes just like genuine Parma ham, or Ibérico *pata negra jamón*. The breeds of pig used to make those hams – as well as their diet, terrain, and climate – are unique. However, if you use high-quality pork from a heritage breed such as Berkshire, Duroc, or Gloucester Old Spot, you will produce a fantastic ham with a quality and flavor that reflects your particular environment.

I always dry cure prosciutto on the bone and slice it in the traditional way. However, I understand that you might want to slice large rounds unobstructed, so I've given instructions on how to remove the bone after curing on pp. 160–63.

Makes 1 prosciutto (about 15.5 lb/7 kg)

A leg of free-range pork, bone in and trotter attached

For the cure

2 (5 lb/25 kg) bags PDV or other additive-free salt (one for submerging the ham in and the other to act as a weight placed on top of the ham)

About 6½ tbsp malt vinegar

Equipment

Heavy-duty scales (up to 22 lb/10 kg)

Large plastic (or wooden) food-grade box and wooden board

Butcher's hook

Jambon sac (optional)

Meat slicer (optional)

(continued

Prosciutto, *continued*

Weigh the leg of pork before you begin, as this determines the length of time it needs to be immersed in the salt. The meat requires 3 days' salting per 2.2 pounds (1 kg). So, for example, a leg weighing 4.4 pounds (5 kg) will need to be in salt for 6 days.

Before you place the leg of pork in the salt, remove any flaps of skin or oxidized parts of meat where blood has coagulated. Try to make the surface of the meat as clean and even as possible. It also pays to massage the leg from the trotter end to the thicker end, as this will release any residual blood that may be left in the femoral artery. Blood has a negative effect in curing meats. Rub the pork with a clean cloth doused in malt vinegar. The main advantage of keeping the trotter on is that you can then hang the leg for air-drying by the Achilles tendon on a butcher's hook. In addition, you won't be exposing an extra bit of flesh, which reduces the risk of spoilage, or attracting flies.

Have your chosen container ready (see p. 100). It is better to have the box in situ now, because, once it contains the ham and salt, it will be a real hernia job trying to move it. The best site for the salting to take place is off the floor in an outbuilding or in a cool, dry larder or pantry.

Pour a layer of salt about 1½ inches deep over the base of the container and place the pork leg on top. Add the rest of the salt, making sure every bit of the leg is covered and it is completely submerged beneath at least 1½ inches of salt. If the leg is particularly large, it may be the case that more salt is required to complete the job. This will look and feel like an excessive amount of salt, but it is a guaranteed ratio that will work. If you use a plastic box, you have the advantage of being able to see if the ham is touching the side of the box, without being surrounded by salt. Lift the leg slightly at that point and allow the salt to encase it by giving it a gentle prod. If you use a wooden box, just make sure there is enough clearance around the leg when you put it in for it to be completely enveloped in the salt.

Find a wooden cutting board that fits neatly inside the box and place it on top of the salt-covered pork. Put a large weight on top. It has to be a significant weight. I use a spare 55-pound (25 kg) bag of salt (still contained in the bag) or an old potato weight (56 pounds) for this purpose. The weight helps drive the cure in as well as give the ham that classic prosciutto shape. Make a note of the date your ham is due to come out of the salt. A day either side of this date may not be too critical to the overall final taste, but try to stick to it.

When you have salted the ham for the allotted time, remove it from the box and wash it thoroughly with fresh cold water to remove the salt. Rub the whole joint with malt vinegar, then hang it in your air-drying spot for up to 12 months. In warm weather, wrap it loosely in a jambon sac (see p. 52) so that flies won't be able to get to t, but the air will be able to move over it and you will still be able to see the ham through the thin fabric. If you wrap it too tightly, it will still allow flies to lay eggs through it. If there is a cold snap, you don't really want the ham to freeze, as it halts the curing process, though that will continue once it warms up again. Freezing is actually unlikely, due to the amount of salt present in the ham, but if temperatures get very low, you might want to move it to a slightly warmer place, or even the fridge.

It is important that the ham doesn't dry too fast or it will be "sealed" on the outside and moisture won't be able to escape, but you do want a crust to gradually form on the outside that will protect it. To keep the drying slow, the ham must not be allowed to get too warm (i.e., go above 84°F). Air circulation is really the most crucial thing. It is no use trying to do this in a stagnant environment, as this will attract the wrong molds.

The first time you do this, let the ham hang for the full 12 months (by which time it should have lost 30 percent of its original weight). Any less than this and you will just be cheating yourself on overall taste.

When it comes to the time to sample your ham, remove it from the cloth, if used. It should be firm and have a covering of mold over it. There may be a slight smell of unpasteurized cheese about it, or something a bit musty. Don't worry about this; it is perfectly normal. I take a nailbrush and dip it in malt vinegar at this point to remove the mold from the area where I want to try the ham – usually from the exposed area of meat near the aitchbone, but it doesn't really matter. The mold won't harm you, but it's not necessarily the best part.

Using a sharp knife, carefully remove the hard, crusty exterior to expose the wonderful meat just underneath. Slice the ham as finely as you can and enjoy its deliciousness as you reflect on the passing year.

Note: Don't add any herbs or spices to the ham before it goes into the salt. It is better to add flavor much later on, after eating some of the cured ham for the first time. After the first slices have been taken off, exposing some of the cured leg, you can create a covering paste consisting of pork lard and flour. The Italians call this a *strutto*, and it acts as a protective barrier, allowing the ham to continue to mature. You can add flavorings such as coriander, chile, and black pepper to this paste. They won't affect the cure but will inform the first few layers of meat underneath the *strutto*.

Variation

sirloin joint proscuitto If you want to practice all of the elements of curing a piece of pork in this way but don't want to go straight to the expense of a whole leg, you can apply the same technique to a sirloin joint. Follow the same method and weight–curing time ratio, but expect it to be ready to eat in around 4 months.

Boning an air-dried ham

Traditionally, Parma and prosciutto hams are cured with the aitchbone removed but with the femur still in. The aitchbone is part of the pelvis that sits on top of the femur bone at the thick end of the leg and creates a classic ball-and-socket joint. It takes a certain amount of skill to remove it but can be done with a bit of patience – or you could ask your butcher to do it for you.

The first time you cure a leg, I would suggest you leave the aitchbone in, because it offers that extra bit of protection and leaves less flesh exposed. However, leaving it in does cause some difficulties later on when it comes to slicing the leg, as it will act as an obstruction. You certainly won't be able to use a meat slicer with the aitchbone still in – nor, for that matter, will you be able to slice lovely large rounds of ham with the femur still running through it. You will just need to get proficient at shaving off shards with a sharp knife – just as they do in Italy and Spain.

To remove the aitchbone before curing, you will need a flexible boning knife to work your way underneath the bone. The technique is illustrated on p. 74. Once you've traced the outline of the aitchbone, it is a matter of prying it away from the femur and connective tissue. To the first timer, this will be difficult, and the addition of working with a sharp knife adds to the jeopardy. Take your time and always make sure the ham is resting steadily against the board. Rather like shucking an oyster, this technique will become second nature with practice.

If you want to create a boneless air-dried ham, perfect for slicing on a meat slicer, you can remove the femur during the drying process at around 6 months. If you attempt to remove the bone too early in the drying process, the ham will never regain its shape and the space created by removing the bone won't close. If you leave it too late, the ham will be so hard that it will be impossible to get the gouge in. Generally the hams that I bone out are 6 to 8 months along their curing journey. This is quite a large window, I know: the best way to judge it is by pressing hard on the outside of your ham and feeling if there is some "give," which slowly comes back to shape after a while. This is the time to bone it.

You will need a butcher's saw and a hand bone gouge, which looks like a large metal shoehorn and has a beveled end and a rounded shaft (pic 1).

With the aitchbone removed before you place the leg in salt, you already have one point of entry for the hand bone gouge. However, you still need to expose and release the other end, which is just above the knee. There is a recognizable point on the cut surface of the leg that indicates where to make the incision. It looks like two small peaks either side of a dip (pic 2). If it isn't apparent to the naked eye, you

Boning an air-dried ham at around 6 months

(continued on next page)

Boning an air-dried ham (continued)

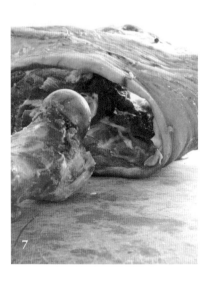

should be able to feel for it. You should be able to make a cut here all the way through the leg so that the knuckle below the knee is removed. Don't worry if this sounds too complicated. You can always choose a point near to where you think the knee is and use the saw to cut through the bone. It's just a bit crude and passes some bone dust around the meat.

With the tip of a knife, start to pry away the flesh at the top end of the femur (pic 3) and at the other end so that you can insert the tip of the gouge. Don't go in too deeply with the knife, as this will cause crisscross marks to run visibly through the meat that will ruin the look of any rounds sliced off.

Now, with some effort, you should be able to force the end of the gouge along the length of the bone (pic 4) in order to separate it from the muscles and pull it free; the shape of the gouge means you won't leave too much meat on the bone. Eventually you should be able to work all around the bone (pic 5) so that it can be removed completely with a bit of a twist and a pull (pic 6). Often the kneecap is still in place, and this should be located and removed. It looks and feels like a hard circular dome just under the skin close to where you made your cut.

Now you have a tunnel where the bone used to be (pic 7). It needs to be sealed up. Don't be tempted to pack this space with salt; it will make your ham far too salty. Instead, devise a way to press the ham so that the gap becomes sealed. At River Cottage, we have specially rigged-up boxes that we use to press hams. They are made from pine and consist of a frame deep enough to hold a big ham with slats top and bottom, which encase the ham. The slats are tightened onto the ham with pieces of wood running across the top and bottom, using two threaded bolts and a couple of wing nuts. This getup is typically River Cottage in the sense it is ever so slightly "rustic," but it absolutely works. In much the same manner, here I've used an apple press (pic 8); two pieces of wood held tightly with clamps would function in the same way. The ham should be ready after 24 hours in the press. You can then carry on air-drying it for the rest of the year as it was.

Goat violin

TECHNIQUES	Dry curing, air-drying
CURING TIME	Minimum 2 months

Goat is such an underestimated meat, with many uses beyond the wonderful currie goat. It can also be a very sustainable and ethical choice. At River Cottage, we ar lucky enough to work with James Whetlor of Cabrito who supplies us with mea from young male goats, by-products of the goat dairy industry. Goats like thes would normally be killed at birth, but when fed up and well looked after, billy goa meat can be a delicacy on a par with rose veal (the corresponding by-product of th bovine dairy industry). Young goat meat is extremely lean, with a milky pinkne and a musky, gamy smell. These notes carry through to the cured meat, although th color becomes darker.

This recipe owes much to a northern Italian prosciutto-style, dry cured recip *violino di capra*. Traditionally the cured goat leg is passed around a table of dine who hold it like a violin and slice off the meat using a long knife as if it were a bow

As goat leg is very lean, it takes a shorter time to cure and dry than a pork le and it needs less salt – just 3 percent of the weight of the leg. This cure method less aggressive than the salt-box method used for a prosciutto ham.

Makes about 2.2 lb/1 kg

1 goat leg, 4.4 to 6.6 lb (2 to 3 kg)

For the cure
About 2.1 oz/60 g PDV or other additive-free salt (i.e., 3 percent of the weight of the goat leg)
½ cup (3.5 oz/100 g) Demerara sugar
4 clove garlics, crushed
1 tbsp (0.35 oz/10 g) juniper berries, bruised

4 tsp (0.42 oz/12 g) black peppercorns, freshly cracked
3 sprigs thyme
3 sprigs rosemary
5 fresh bay leaves

Equipment
Ziplock food bag
Food-grade tray
Butcher's hook and string
Meat slicer (optional)

For the cure, mix all the ingredients together in a bowl. Put the goat leg in a ziplock food bag and pour the cure over it. Seal the bag. Make sure the leg covered on all sides with the cure, and if the femur bone is exposed at the top en ay particular attention to getting some cure in and around the ball of the bone. Massage the cure into the meat, making sure it is evenly distributed.

Place the ziplock bag in a tray or suitable container and leave to cure in the fridge, allowing 1 day for every 2.2 pounds (1 kg). The leg should be massaged or at least turned once or twice in order to redistribute the cure.

After the allotted curing time, remove the goat leg from the bag and rinse off the cure under a cold running tap. Pat it dry with a clean tea towel. Discard the liquid that has collected in the ziplock bag. Once cured, the leg should feel firmer and have a darker hue to it.

Now hang the goat leg in suitable air-drying conditions (see p. 103), with a good flow of air, 60 to 80 percent humidity, and a temperature that is somewhere between 0°F and 64°F, for 2 to 5 months.

Serve the cured goat thinly sliced, like a prosciutto, with figs.

Variation

lamb violin A fairly small leg of lamb, weighing 4.4 to 6.6 pounds (2 to 3 kg), can be used instead of the goat leg for this recipe.

Salami

TECHNIQUES	Fermentation, air-drying
CURING TIME	Minimum 6 weeks

This method of curing meat is perhaps the oldest. The meat is allowed to ferment and dry out over a period of time, resulting in a form of sausage that doesn't need cooking. The cure is integrated fully with the meat, rather than being applied to the surface, so the meat needs to be ground or finely chopped to allow the cure to work effectively. The ratio of salt to the overall weight of the other ingredients must be a minimum of 2 percent in order to cure the meat effectively but not much more than this to avoid oversalting.

The full technique for filling and tying salami is described and illustrated on pp. 88–92. It is simple enough, but easier if you get someone to help you.

Makes about 10 salami

several lengths of beef rounds or
   beef middle casings
5.7 lb (2.6 kg) boneless shoulder or
   picnic shoulder of free-range pork
14 oz (400 g) fatback (see p. 81)
1 or 2 cloves garlic, very finely chopped
1½ tbsp (1.4 oz/40 g) black peppercorns,
   freshly cracked

1 to 2 glasses of red wine
2.1 oz (60 g) PDV or other
   additive-free salt

Equipment
Meat grinder
Sausage stuffer
Butcher's hooks and string
Meat slicer (optional)

Soak the casings for at least 2 hours in cold water.

Grind the pork using the coarse (⅓ to ⅜ inch) plate of your grinder and place in a bowl. Cut the fatback into ¹⁄₁₆-inch dice and add to the meat. Now add the garlic, cracked pepper, wine, and salt. Mix the ingredients together thoroughly by hand.

Pack the mixture into the barrel of your sausage stuffer and fit a medium nozzle on the end. Load the casing onto the sausage stuffer, tie the end with string, and fill the casing as described and shown on pp. 88–92, to form sausages about 12 inches long, packing tightly and ensuring there are no air pockets. Secure the other end of the casing with a second piece of string.

(continued)

Salami, *continued*

The natural casings are inclined to bow into a horseshoe shape. I tie the string at the ends of the salami into loops, then slip both loops onto one hook and hang them like this. However, if you prefer straight salami, suspend them from one end only and they will straighten up. To begin with, you will need to hang the salami in a warm place, ideally 77°F to 81°F, to enable incubation of the bacteria and facilitate fermentation.

After 12 hours in this environment, move the salami to your dry curing spot which should be between 54°F and 64°F with a humidity level of around 70 percent and a constant circulation of air (see p. 103). Make sure the salami are not touching a wall or one another and are not in direct sunlight. Over the coming weeks, test the pH to ensure it is below 4.5. A white mold should form on the casings indicating that this level has been reached.

The salami may take anywhere from 6 to 10 weeks to mature, depending on the conditions and, indeed, on how you like them. They can be sampled as soon as they are fairly firm to the touch and dry looking, but they will continue to dry out and harden until they are practically rock hard.

When the salami reach the stage you like, wipe off any mold from the outside with a cloth soaked in vinegar, then rub the surface with a little olive oil. Transfer the salami to the fridge.

Serve your salami in slices ¹⁄₁₆ to ⅛ inch thick. If you prefer, peel off the ring of casing from each slice before eating, although it is perfectly safe to eat.

Variations

Fennel seeds and grated orange zest make a wonderful addition to this mix and go really well with the pork. Alternatively, try them in a venison salami: in this case you still have to include some pork fat in the mix, as venison is a very lean meat. A ratio of 3 parts venison to 1 part pork fat works well.

Chorizo

TECHNIQUES	Fermentation, air-drying
CURING TIME	Minimum 6 weeks

There are probably hundreds of recipes for chorizo. Throughout the Iberian Peninsula, as well as Latin America, families have been handing down their own recipes for generations. The meat is flavored with a spice mix, usually largely informed by paprika, but which can also include fiery cayenne or naga chile, which will send it off the Scoville scale (the scale used to measure chile heat).

This recipe is for a salami-style chorizo, made with a fairly eclectic blend of spices that can be altered to suit your own heat threshold. It also includes pieces of cured loin of pork, which provide a nice contrast, both texturally and visually. I've added smoked paprika to the mix, to give it a more subtle smokiness. Alternatively, you could use ordinary paprika and cold smoke the salami yourself (see p. 114), after it has had 2 weeks or so of normal air-drying.

Makes about 20 medium chorizo

3 or 4 lengths of beef round casings

11 lb (5 kg) boneless shoulder or picnic shoulder of free-range pork, with about 20 percent fat (measured roughly by eye)

2.2 lb (1 kg) cured pork loin (see Canadian bacon variation, p. 142)

3.5 oz (100 g) PDV or other additive-free salt (i.e., 2 percent of the weight of the pork)

1 cup plus 2 tbsp (4.4 oz/125 g) smoked hot paprika

⅔ cup (2.5 oz/70 g) sweet paprika (unsmoked)

Scant 3 tbsp (0.52 oz/15 g) cayenne pepper

Rounded ½ cup (1.8 oz/50 g) fennel seeds, lightly toasted

10 clove garlics, finely chopped

1 to 2 glasses of red wine

Equipment

Meat grinder

Sausage stuffer

Butcher's hooks and string

Meat slicer (optional)

Soak the casings for at least 2 hours in cold water.

Grind the pork using the coarse (⅓ to ⅜ inch) plate of your grinder and place in a bowl. Cut the pork loin into small cubes and add to the ground meat with all of

(continued)

Chorizo, *continued*

the other ingredients except the wine. Mix thoroughly, using your hands, so that the flavorings are well distributed throughout the mixture. Now add enough wine to bind the mixture (but not too much, or it will leach out of the skins later, carrying flavor with it along with some of the crucial salt).

Pack the mixture into the sausage stuffer and fit a medium nozzle on the end. Load the casing on to the sausage stuffer, tie the end with string, and fill the casing as described and shown on pp. 88–92 to form sausages about 12 inches long, packing tightly and ensuring there are no air pockets. Secure the other end of the casing with string.

To begin with, you will need to hang the chorizo in a warm place, ideally 77°F to 81°F, to enable incubation of the bacteria and facilitate fermentation.

After 12 hours in this environment, move the chorizo to your dry curing spot, which should be between 54°F and 64°F with a humidity level of approximately 70 percent and a constant circulation of air (see p. 103). Make sure the chorizo are not touching a wall or one another and are not in direct sunlight. Over the coming weeks, test the pH to ensure it is below 4.5. Allow 6 to 10 weeks for the chorizo to cure if you want to eat it raw. Serve cut into thin slices.

Note: Should you want to, you can cook with the chorizo soon after mixing rather than leave it to cure. Try crumbling it over fish before baking or putting it into casings and cooking like a sausage to serve with scrambled eggs. There will be an extra saltiness to it, but not to its detriment. Just hold back on additional seasonings in the dish you are preparing.

Chorizo Scotch egg

This is a brilliant way to use up any leftover chorizo mix. Boil a large egg for 5 minutes and allow it to cool. Shell the egg, wrap it in a portion of chorizo mix, and roll it in flour, beaten egg, and bread crumbs, respectively. Deep-fry in hot oil for 5 minutes, until golden brown. On slicing it open, the pork should be cooked through and the egg yolk still runny.

Cotechino

TECHNIQUES	Fermentation, air-drying
CURING TIME	Minimum 5 days

Making this Italian cured sausage is a labor of love because it involves dicing a considerable amount of fatback and pork rind into small pieces, which is a fairly tricky operation. The fat slips in your fingers and the rind is tough and difficult to cut, but it is definitely worth the effort. The meat should carry a good amount of fat, with additional finely chopped pork rind mixed in. I like to use the rind from a piece of bacon, or the skin removed from an aged piece of *lardo* (see p. 151); the mix of fatty flavors gives a wonderful salty-sticky quality to the cured sausage. This classic recipe is adapted from *The River Cottage Meat Book*.

Makes 3 or 4 cotechino

Natural sausage casings: for a salami-
   style cotechino use beef middles
   (2 to 4 inches wide); for a larger
   haggis-style cotechino use
   beef bung (about 6 inches wide)
2 lb (1 kg) boneless shoulder or
   picnic shoulder of free-range pork
14 oz (400 g) fatback (see p. 81)
1.3 lb (600 g) pork rind

For the cure
1.8 oz (50 g) fine salt
1 glass of red wine
4 cloves garlic, finely chopped

1 tsp black or mixed peppercorns,
   freshly ground
A few gratings of fresh nutmeg
1 tsp ground cinnamon
3 or 4 cloves, ground
1 tsp ground mace
A good pinch of dried thyme
4 dried bay leaves

Equipment
Meat grinder
Sausage stuffer
Butcher's hooks and string

Soak the sausage casings overnight in cold water.

Grind the meat using the coarse (⅓ to ⅜ inch) plate of your grinder and place in a bowl. Dice the pork fat and rind into small pieces, add to the meat, and mix well.

Mix the cure ingredients together in a bowl. Add the combined meat, fat, and rind and mix thoroughly by hand.

(continued)

Cotechino, *continued*

Pack the mixture into the sausage stuffer and fit a medium nozzle on the end. Load the casing onto the sausage stuffer, tie the end with string, and fill the casing as shown and described on pp. 88–92, to form sausages about 4 inches long, packing the mixture tightly and ensuring there are no air pockets. Secure the other end of the casing with string.

Hang the cotechino in a dry, airy place, such as a drafty outbuilding or covered porch, making sure they do not touch a wall or one another (see p. 103). They will be ready to cook and eat after about 5 days but are perhaps at their best at 15 to 20 days. By about 40 days, they will be pretty dry and hard.

If you wish to keep the cotechino any longer, vacuum seal or wrap in plastic wrap and refrigerate, and they will keep for another month or so. Alternatively, freeze them for up to a year.

To cook a cotechino, immerse it fully in a pan of cold water and slowly bring to a simmer. Cook gently for about 1½ hours for thin sausages (i.e., stuffed middles) or 2½ hours for fat ones (i.e., stuffed bung).

Drain the cotechino and cut into thick slices. It is delicious served hot on a bed of warm Puy lentils dressed with olive oil, salt, and pepper.

Sichuan-cured pork loin

TECHNIQUES	Dry curing, air-drying
CURING TIME	Minimum 4 days

This uses a boneless loin of pork with a layer of fatback still attached – essentially [a] rack of invertebrate pork chops. The loin can be cured as a whole or in shorter sections. The curing time will be the same whatever the length, as it is the thickness, not length, that determines how long it needs in the cure. This cure is inspired by my friend Mark Diacono, who grows his own Sichuan pepper.

Makes about 50 slices

2.2 lb (1 kg) piece boneless free-range
   pork loin, with a layer of fatback

For the cure

1 oz (30 g) coarse sea salt
5½ tbsp (1.8 oz/50 g) Sichuan pepper,
   roughly ground
3½ tbsp (1 oz/30 g) black peppercorns,
   toasted and cracked

Equipment
Ziplock food bag
Food-grade tray
Butcher's hooks and string

Mix all the ingredients for the cure together in a bowl. Put the pork loin into [a] ziplock bag and add the cure, massaging it all over the meat. Seal the bag, excluding as much air as possible. Place the bag on a tray or in the salad drawer of your fridge.

Leave the pork to cure in the fridge for 3 days per 2.2 pounds (1 kg), giving it a gentle massage to redistribute the cure evenly every day. After the allotted time, remove the pork from the bag and wash off the cure under cold running water. Pat the meat dry and allow it to dry completely. Putting it, uncovered, in the fridge overnight is a good way to do this. It is now ready to slice and fry (like Canadian bacon).

For more pepper flavor, dust the surface of the cured loin with extra Sichuan and black pepper. Tie along the joint using the butcher's knot (see pp. 148–49) and hang it in your air-drying spot (see p. 103) for 3 to 4 weeks, until it has lost 30 percent of its original weight. It can then be served raw, in thin slices.

Variation
Filletto For a quicker version, use pork tenderloin (a mini loin without fat).

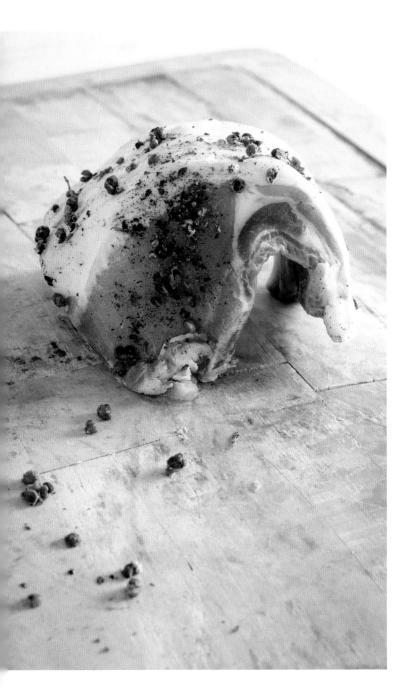

Mortadella

TECHNIQUE	Poaching (no curing)
COOKING TIME	Minimum 50 minutes

Instead of being air-dried, this emulsified sausage is poached and cooled before slicing. This recipe is from my friend Robin Rea of Rusty Pig.

Makes 1 mortadella

1 beef middle casing
1.1 lb (500 g) boneless free-range pork belly
1.1 lb (500 g) fatback (see p. 81)
2 cloves garlic, minced
2½ tsp (0.52 oz/15 g) coarse sea salt
1 tsp black peppercorns, freshly ground
1 tsp ground mace
½ tsp freshly grated nutmeg
½ tsp ground coriander

Scant 3½ tbsp (0.88 oz/25 g) shelled pistachio nuts

Equipment
Meat grinder
Sausage stuffer
Butcher's string
Meat thermometer

Soak the beef casing overnight in cold water.

Grind the belly and fatback separately through the fine (⅛ inch) plate of the grinder.

Put the belly in a bowl and add the garlic, salt, pepper, mace, nutmeg, and coriander. Mix thoroughly, then pass again through the fine plate on the grinder. Place the seasoned meat and the fat in a bowl and refrigerate for at least 30 minutes.

Put the chilled meat and fat into a food processor and process until smooth, then transfer the mixture to a chilled bowl and mix in the pistachios.

Pack the mix into the sausage stuffer and fit the widest nozzle on the end. Load the beef casing onto the sausage stuffer, tie off with a double knot, and fill the casing so it has no air gaps, then secure the other end as shown and described on pp. 88–92.

Lower the sausage into a pot of water and heat slowly. Cook below simmering at about 167°F) for 45 minutes to 1 hour. The internal temperature of the mortadella should reach 149°F, which you can measure with a meat thermometer.

Meanwhile, fill a large bowl with cold water and ice cubes. Remove the cooked mortadella from the pan and immerse in the ice bath to cool quickly, then drain. Serve the mortadella cut into thin slices. It will keep in the fridge for a week.

Guanciale

TECHNIQUES	Dry curing, air-drying
CURING TIME	Minimum 4 weeks

The first time I tried this dry cured, air-dried pig's cheek, it was simply fried in it own juices with a splash of balsamic vinegar. It has made a lasting impression on me and whenever I think about curing meat, memories of that first tasting always come to mind, like a marked page in a well-thumbed book.

The jowl of a pig is a wonderful cut. Combining fat and lean meat, it is soft and yielding before curing (*guanciale* translates as "pillow"), but, once cured, it takes o firmness and incredible character. It can be used to flavor soups, stews, and past sauces, like bacon, or sliced thinly and eaten raw like pancetta.

Sadly, because there appears to be a real stumbling block when it comes to "fac meat," the majority of meat from a pig's head is used to make pet food. Perhaps i makes the link between living animal and food on the plate all too clear for some. prefer to make the best use of those cuts and to be upfront about what they are. A River Cottage, we've taken to referring to this particular product as "face bacon" t really hammer it home.

Makes about 60 slices

2 pig's cheeks, about 2.2 lb (1 kg) in total

For the cure

About 1 oz (300 g) PDV or other additive-free salt (i.e., 3 percent of the weight of the pig's cheeks)
7 tbsp (2.1 oz/60 g) black peppercorns, freshly cracked

Equipment
Kitchen blowtorch (optional)
Ziplock food bag
Food-grade tray
Butcher's hooks

First you need to burn away any residual hair on the pig's cheeks. Singe the cheek with a kitchen blowtorch or over a gas burner, then scrape away the burned hair wit a knife.

Now remove any glands from around the back of the cheeks. They are part of th lymphatic system (which cleans the blood) and won't do you any harm if eaten, bu they are grayish, mushy, and unappealing.

Mix the ingredients for the cure together in a bowl, then transfer to a ziplock bag.

Put the cheeks into the bag and distribute the cure evenly, so that it covers them. Squeeze out as much air as possible, seal the bag, and place on a plastic tray.

Place the tray in the fridge. Let the cheeks cure, allowing 3 days per 1.1 pounds (500 g) – in this case, 6 days – redistributing the cure once or twice as it becomes more liquid.

Remove the cheeks and wash off the cure under cold running water, then pat them dry with a clean tea towel. I like to then dust the dry cured cheeks with more cracked black pepper.

Hang the cured pig's cheeks on butcher's hooks to air-dry in appropriate conditions (see p. 103) for 3 to 5 weeks.

When ready, remove the rind and slice the guanciale thinly to eat raw, cut into pieces to add to soups, stews, and pasta sauces, or fry slices like bacon slices.

Variations

For a sweeter flavor, use the basic River Cottage dry cure (see p. 96). This recipe also works exceptionally well with duck breasts, using the same ratios and timings to create a wonderful duck prosciutto.

Spalla and speck

TECHNIQUES	Dry curing, cold smoking (optional), air-drying
CURING TIME	Minimum 6 months

This might sound like a sequel TV series starring the offspring of Mork and Mindy, but it is in fact is a wonderful duo of cured meats produced from the same cut of pork, the difference being that *speck* is cold smoked and *spalla* is not. Their flavors are quite distinct – the smokiness of *speck* originating from the traditional storage of cured meat in chimneys during the warmer months.

Spalla is traditionally made by keeping the cut on the bone, but I like to remove the bone first so it can easily be sliced. It is very much like dry cured, air-dried ham (see p. 156) but with the bonus of being ready to eat sooner. It will have the look and texture of a prosciutto, but because of its accelerated ascent to curedom, it won't carry the same complex flavors. However, it will still taste wonderful.

Speck shares the same start in life as *spalla*, but after boning and curing, it is cold smoked before air-drying. It is considered to be less refined than a dry cured ham because it comes from the forequarter of the pig, not the leg, but I love it – especially its complex spice and herb flavors applied through the cure.

Makes 1 spalla or speck (about 6.2 lb/2.8 kg)

1 boneless shoulder of free-range
    pork, about 8.8 lb (4 kg)

For the cure

About 4.2 oz (120 g) fine sea salt
    (i.e., 3 percent of the weight of the
    pork shoulder)
½ tsp dry English mustard
½ tsp freshly grated nutmeg
6 tbsp (1.8 oz/50 g) juniper berries,
    finely ground

6 tbsp (1.8 oz/50 g) allspice, freshly
    ground
6 tbsp (1.8 oz/50 g) black peppercorns,
    freshly ground
6 tbsp (3 oz/85 g) packed dark brown
    sugar
10 bay leaves, shredded

Equipment

Ziplock food bag
Butcher's hooks and string
Cold smoker for speck

Place the meat, skin side down, on a board and remove any flaps of loose skin or meat. You are looking to get the surface of the meat as even as possible so it will cure at a uniform rate.

(continued)

Spalla and speck, *continued*

Mix all of the cure ingredients together in a bowl. Grab half of the cure and scatter it in the bottom of a ziplock bag. Place the pork, skin side down, on top, then apply the rest of the cure, massaging it gently into the meat and making sure that the sides are also covered. Seal the ziplock bag.

Leave the meat to cure in a cool place for the equivalent of 3 days per 2.2 pounds (1 kg) weight. If you can find room in your fridge, all the better. Redistribute the cure in the bag every other day so that it is kept in close proximity to the meat.

After the allotted time (12 days for an 8.8-pound [4 kg] shoulder), wash the cure off the meat under cold running water and pat it dry with a clean tea towel. Allow the meat to sit in the fridge for a day or so.

Roll and tie along the joint using the butcher's knot (see pp. 148–49).

If you want to make speck, at this stage fire up your cold smoker and cold smoke the meat gently for 4 to 8 hours.

Either way – smoked or not – air-dry the meat as you would an air-dried ham (see pp. 158–59) until it has lost 30 percent of its original weight, which can take anywhere from 6 to 12 months. Serve spalla or speck cut into thin slices.

Venison biltong

TECHNIQUES	Dry curing, wet curing, air-drying
CURING TIME	Minimum 10 days

This flavor-packed cured snack from South Africa is pretty close to jerky in it method. It is quite brittle and hard to begin with but, after a few challenging chews, it starts to soften and relent, allowing all those fantastic flavors to fill you mouth. On the odd occasion when the River Cottage team is allowed out of the county, we can often be seen munching on sticks of home-cured *biltong* on the train to London.

Makes 4 to 6 strips

A whole small or ½ large haunch of venison

For the cure

2 tbsp PDV or other additive-free salt

2 tbsp soft dark brown sugar

1 tbsp coriander seeds, roasted and ground

1 tbsp black peppercorns, freshly cracked

3 tbsp malt vinegar

Equipment

Food-grade tray

Butcher's hooks and string

Prepare the meat by seaming out (i.e., dividing) the leg into individual muscles Use only the meat that you can clearly define as being long grained (the rest is idea for salami).

Using a sharp knife, slice the meat along the grain into long steaks about ⅛ inch thick, removing any sinew and fat as you go. You need 1.1 pounds (500 g) meat. leg will give you more than you require, so divide the rest into batches and freez it for future biltong making or for venison salami.

For the cure, mix the salt, sugar, coriander, and cracked pepper together thorough in a bowl. Scatter a layer of this cure mixture evenly in a large food-grade tray, the add the venison steaks. Cover the meat evenly with the remaining cure, rubbin it in well. Now add the malt vinegar, sprinkling it evenly over both sides of th venison steaks.

Cover the tray and place in the fridge. Allow to cure for 6 hours, turning the meat and rubbing in the mixture again after 2 hours.

Remove the meat from the tray. Shake off any loose seasoning and carefully pat the meat dry with a tea towel. Hang each strip of biltong individually from a hook, using a piece of string. Leave to dry in a cool, dry, dark, and airy place (at 50°F) until semidried – about 10 days.

You can then finish your biltong off in a very low oven. I am fortunate to have a wonderful Esse stove at home, which has two oven compartments, and I hang the biltong strips in the bottom warming oven, using butcher's hooks. If your stove doesn't have a warming oven, hang the meat from the top shelf of your oven on its lowest setting. If you think that may still be too hot, leave the oven door slightly open. It will take 4 to 6 hours to dry. When finished, the biltong should be so dry that it will splinter when bent in two.

Alternatively, if the weather permits – that is, if it's hot, dry, and sunny with a good flow of air – the biltong can be fully dried outside (see p. 103).

Store the biltong wrapped in waxed paper. It will keep for 2 to 3 weeks if semidried and for up to 2 years when fully dried.

Bresaola

TECHNIQUES	Dry curing, wet curing, air-drying
CURING TIME	Minimum 19 days

This recipe is adapted from *The River Cottage Meat Book* and is a truly wonderful way to deal with a joint of beef that, to my mind, is all too often turned into an inferior roast. Beef that has been through this magical, aromatic, boozy baptism turns a deep purple on the outside, and thin slices of it – arranged on a platter and finished with a drizzle of olive oil – look like beautiful stained-glass windows.

The method starts off with a dredging of dry cure and then a good drenching in a cold red-wine bath before air-drying.

Serves about 30 (a few slices each)

A joint of beef bottom round or top round, about 8.8 lb (4 kg)

For the cure
About 4.2 oz (120 g) coarse sea salt (i.e., 3 percent of the weight of the beef)
12 sprigs rosemary
12 bay leaves, torn
20 cloves
4 cloves garlic, crushed

1 tbsp black peppercorns, freshly cracked
2 tbsp dried chile flakes
5 or 6 strips finely pared orange zest
5 or 6 strips finely pared lemon zest
1 (750 ml) bottle red wine

Equipment
Food-grade container
Butcher's hooks and string

Trim the outside of the meat, removing any fat or sinews.

Mix together all the dry ingredients for the cure and place in a food-grade container into which the joint will fit quite snugly.

Add the meat, turning it to coat well. This way of applying the cure mix is often called "dredging." Cover and leave in a cool place – the fridge if you like – for 4 days, turning the meat every other day.

Pour the bottle of wine over the meat, or at least enough wine to virtually cover the meat, and return to the fridge. Turn the meat once a day for 5 days, then remove it from the marinade and pat dry with a clean tea towel (though not one that carries any sentimental value, as it will get badly stained).

Tie up the meat with string, using the butcher's knot (see pp. 148–49), and hang it in a dry, cool, and drafty place such as an outbuilding, covered porch, or poorly made shed (see p. 103) – or put it in the fridge – for at least 10 days, but closer to 4 weeks for a more traditional finish.

When ready, it should be fairly hard to the touch on the surface but the center will be silky smooth and slightly giving. The bresaola might need to be trimmed of the hard discolored exterior before slicing, especially if it has hung for a longer period. Slice it very thinly, across the grain of the meat, like a giant salami.

A finished bresaola can be hung in a cool place for up to a month and used as and when you need it. In warm or humid weather, transfer it to the fridge.

Lamb culatello

TECHNIQUES	Dry curing–wet curing hybrid, air-drying
CURING TIME	Minimum 5 months

I have taken some liberties with this method but it is with the best intentions. The term *culatello* traditionally refers to the boned back half of a pig's hind leg that has been sewn up in a pig's bladder and cured for up to 4 years. My version uses the same set of muscles from a boned leg of lamb but does away with the bladder, replacing it with a beef bung casing. It came about as a result of my attempts to find a good way to cure a leg of lamb. Ready to eat within just 5 to 6 months, the recipe is a great example of how you can apply a traditional method in a new way to create something different but, to my mind, of equal excellence.

Makes 1 culatello (serves about 10)

1 beef bung casing
1 boned, skinned, and rolled rump of halved lamb leg (the largest muscle from the rear top part of the leg, shank removed), 2.2 to 4.4 lb (1 to 2 kg)

For the cure

1 to 2.1 oz (30 to 60 g) PDV salt (i.e., 3 percent of the weight of the lamb)
1 tsp chopped rosemary

½ tsp chopped thyme
½ glass of red wine

Equipment
Ziplock food bag
Butcher's hooks and string

Soak the beef bung casing overnight in cold water.

Put the piece of lamb into a ziplock food bag.

For the cure, mix the salt with the herbs and add to the bag, then pour in the red wine. Seal the bag and place on a tray or other container so that the liquid doesn't spill, should it leak from the bag. Refrigerate for 1 day per 2.2 pounds (1 kg) of lamb.

After the allotted time, remove the lamb from the bag, rinse, and pat dry. Place the lamb in the casing. This might at first be a tight squeeze, but eventually it should fit. Tie the length of the encased lamb using the butcher's knot (see pp. 148–49).

Air-dry the cured lamb (see p. 103) for 5 months, until it's lost 30 percent of its original weight. It will be dry throughout but with a tender texture. Thinly slice to serve.

Cider-cured ham

TECHNIQUES	Wet curing, air-drying, cold smoking (optional)
CURING TIME	Minimum 15 days

There are few better partnerships than pork and apple. There are even fewer better than pork and cider, a bit of old English alchemy. This recipe can be applied to a whole leg of pork, weighing 2.2 pounds (10 kg) or more, but you can use a smaller portion off the bone, as I prefer to do, or even sirloin. The quantities here are for a small, whole boned-out leg or half a large leg.

Serves 6 to 8

1 whole or ½ leg of free-range
    pork, boned and chilled

For the brine
2.4 lb (1.1 kg) PDV salt
4½ cups pressed apple juice
    (i.e., not from concentrate)
4½ cups strong dry hard cider
10¾ cups water
4½ cups (2.2 lb/1 kg) Demerara sugar
4½ cups (2.2 lb/1 kg) packed dark
    brown sugar

20 to 30 juniper berries
3½ tbsp (1 oz/30 g) black peppercorns,
    crushed
10 bay leaves, crushed
10 cloves

Equipment
Food-grade brine tub
Food-grade tray
Cold smoker (optional)

Put all the ingredients for the brine into a large saucepan, bring to a boil, and leave to cool. Transfer to a food-grade brine tub and chill to 37°F to 39°F.

Weigh your piece of pork, then place it in the tub and submerge it completely in the brine, using a food-grade tray with a weight on top. Leave the pork in the brine, in the coolest place you can find if the tub is too large for your fridge, for a minimum of 3 days (or maximum of 4 days) for every 2.2 pounds (1 kg). The minimum time will suffice if you plan to cook and eat the ham soon after it has finished curing, but you should use the maximum time if you intend to keep it longer.

After its allotted time, remove the ham from the cure, wipe it dry with a cotton cloth, and hang it to dry in a well-ventilated cool place for 24 hours.

(continued)

Cider-cured ham, *continued*

You can then cold smoke it if you like: hang it high above a hardwood fire or put it in your cold smoker and either smoke it continuously for 24 hours or intermittently (6 to 12 hours a day) for 2 to 4 days. The ideal air temperature where the ham is smoking is 81°F; a little variation won't hurt, but it should not exceed 104°F.

Smoked or unsmoked, this ham keeps well if you go for the maximum cure time: hang it in a well-ventilated outbuilding, or covered porch where a draft can get to it but the rain can't (see p. 103), and it should keep right through the winter months. In warmer weather, hams are at risk from flies and other bugs, so it's best to get them cooked before too long. A minimum-cure-time unsmoked ham should be kept in the fridge, wrapped in a cloth or cheesecloth, but not plastic wrap, and cooked within a month of curing.

Cooking your ham

I've read a lot of recipes that suggest hams should be soaked in plenty of fresh water which is changed every 12 hours, for 24 to 48 hours, depending on the length of the cure, before boiling. I don't subscribe to this – it smacks of not getting the original cure right. If you draw the moisture out and drive the salty cure in, then undo part of this by soaking it in water, the ham won't know whether it's coming or going.

Instead, put your ham in a large cooking pot, cover with water, bring to a boil, and simmer very gently for 2 to 5 hours, depending on size. If the water tastes very salty after the first hour of cooking, pour at least half of it away and top up with fresh boiling water from the kettle. When the fat starts to separate from the meat, it should be ready.

You can either serve the ham simply boiled (I love it as a pared-down meal with boiled spuds and a dollop of mustard) or add a further stage of baking, which is what I tend to do when I serve it as a festive centerpiece on Boxing Day: remove the ham from the cooking liquid and allow it to cool slightly. Preheat the oven to 350°F. Slice the skin off the ham and score the fat in a diamond pattern. Mix ⅓ cup (3.5 oz/100 g) honey with 2 tablespoons dry English mustard and smear it over the ham. Place in the oven for 40 minutes to 1 hour, depending on size, until caramelized. Serve hot or at room temperature. Sumptuous.

Note: There is an alternative method for brining, using a brine pump. Instead of submerging the product in the brine you use a pump to inject the brine into the product. I find this method too hit or miss, as it doesn't give a uniform result. And it doesn't work at all on anything smaller than a large chicken.

Pressed beef tongue

TECHNIQUE	Wet curing
CURING TIME	Minimum 3 days

Often mistaken for an organ and categorized as offal, tongue is in fact a muscle. It may not currently be on your top-ten ingredients list, but, with a little effort, this cut of meat can be transformed into something tasty for the whole family.

Serves 10

1 beef tongue

For the brine
8½ cups water
1.1 lb (500 g) PDV or other
    additive-free salt
1 tsp dried chile flakes

1 clove
2 dried bay leaves
½ tsp white peppercorns

Equipment
Food-grade brine tub

Put all of the ingredients for the brine into a large saucepan and stir well. Place over low heat until the salt is fully dissolved, then bring to a boil and let bubble for 1 to 2 minutes. Remove from the heat and allow to cool completely.

Place the tongue in a food-grade brine tub, such as a large plastic box, and cover completely with the brine. Weigh the tongue down with a weight placed on a tray or plate so that it is fully submerged. Leave in a cool place for 1 day per 2.2 pounds (1 kg).

Remove the tongue from the brine and rinse thoroughly in cold water. Put it into a saucepan and cover with fresh cold water. Bring to a simmer and cook gently for 3 to 4 hours, until the tongue is really tender. Allow it to cool slightly in the liquid.

When the tongue is cool enough to handle, lift it out of the pan and peel away the coarse skin. Put the tongue into a basin or terrine in which it fits quite snugly. Pour on a little of the cooking liquid (which will set like a jelly as it chills). Place a small plate on top of the tongue and put a heavy weight on top. Allow it to cool completely and then refrigerate for 2 days.

Turn the pressed tongue out of the bowl (it may be necessary to immerse the bowl in warm water to release the tongue). Serve it thinly sliced, with assorted pickles.

Salt beef

TECHNIQUE	Wet curing
CURING TIME	Minimum 2 days

This classic method for making delicious open-textured salt beef is adapted from *The River Cottage Meat Book*. You can also use it to cook a beef tongue. Conventional wisdom has it that the best cuts for salt beef are bottom round and brisket, the former being much superior. I have experimented with various cuts, including fore shank and even a large chunk of shank on the bone. They all work well, but in my book the fattiest, cheapest cuts give the most open-grained texture, which is what I like. So I stick to brisket and fore shank for this recipe – both usually on the bone. I tend to keep the leaner bottom round for the Italian dry cured beef, *bresaola*.

Serves 10 or more

4.4 to 6.6 lb (2 to 3 kg) piece beef brisket or fore shank (or use a whole beef tongue)

For the brine

5½ qts water
2.2 lb (1 kg) PDV or other additive-free salt
3 cups (1.3 lb/600 g) Demerara or packed light brown sugar
1 tsp black peppercorns
1 tsp juniper berries
5 cloves
4 bay leaves
1 sprig thyme

To cook the beef

1 bouquet garni
1 carrot, peeled and chopped
1 onion, chopped
1 celery stalk, chopped
1 leek, chopped
½ head garlic (sliced horizontally to cut through the cloves)

Equipment

Food-grade brine tub
Food-grade tray

Put all the ingredients for the brine into a large saucepan and place over low heat stirring occasionally until the salt and sugar have fully dissolved. Bring to a boil and allow to bubble for 1 to 2 minutes, then remove from the heat and allow the brine to cool completely.

Put your chosen piece of beef into a food-grade brine tub and cover it completely with the brine. Weigh the meat down if necessary with a weight placed on a tray or a piece of wood to keep it submerged.

Leave the piece of beef to cure in a cool place for 1 day per 2.2 pounds (1 kg), then remove it from the brine.

To cook the beef, put it into a saucepan with the bouquet garni, vegetables, and garlic. Cover with fresh water and bring to a gentle simmer. Poach it very gently on the stove top or in the oven (preheated to 300°F) if you prefer. Cook until the meat is completely tender and yielding when pierced with a skewer. A 6.6-pound (3 kg) piece of beef will take 2½ to 3 hours.

Serve the hot salt beef carved into fairly thick slices, with lentils, beans, or boiled potatoes and either creamed fresh horseradish or good English mustard. Alternatively, you can serve it cold. It will keep for a further week in prime condition; thereafter it will begin to dry out too much.

Note: If you've cured a beef tongue rather than a piece of beef, you will need to peel off the coarse skin before serving.

Beer-brined smoked beef heart

TECHNIQUE	Wet curing
CURING TIME	Minimum 24 hours

My mum used to cook a stuffed beef heart, which was amazing. The closest thing I've had to it was made in the River Cottage kitchen by sous chef Andy Tyrell. I've combined elements of both dishes here, which hopefully does them proud.

Serves 4 to 6

1 beef heart, trimmed of all excess fat
   and connective tissue

For the brine

5½ cups dark beer or stout

6.3 oz (180 g) PDV or other additive-
   free salt

1 cup plus 2 tbsp (8.8 oz/250 g) packed
   dark brown sugar

¼ cup (1.8 oz/50 g) Demerara sugar

3 bay leaves

2 star anise pods

1 cinnamon stick

For the stuffing

8.8 oz (250 g) bacon offcuts, finely diced

1 small onion, finely diced

1 or 2 cloves garlic, crushed

1 cup (1.8 oz/50 g) fresh bread crumbs

2 tbsp finely chopped sage

A good pinch of freshly grated nutmeg

Salt and freshly ground black pepper

To cook the beef

1 tbsp beef drippings or olive oil

2 onions, sliced

4 or 5 carrots, peeled

1 or 2 cloves garlic, chopped

For the brine, set aside 2 cups of the beer (for the stuffing and cooking), then put the remaining 4½ cups in a stockpot with all the other brine ingredients. Bring to a boil, stirring to dissolve the salt and sugar. Allow the brine to cool right down and refrigerate it. Place the beef heart in the brine and leave in the fridge for 24 hours.

For the stuffing, mix all the ingredients in a bowl, with a small glass of the reserved beer, until well combined. Slice the heart horizontally into large, more or less rectangular pieces. In each, put a teaspoonful or two of the stuffing mix. Roll up to make large "hearty" parcels, and secure with wooden skewers to hold the stuffing in.

To cook, heat the drippings in a pot over medium heat and fry the onions, carrots, and garlic until well colored, then add the rest of the held-back beer. Cook gently, on the stove top or in the oven (preheated to 325°F), for 2½ to 3 hours, until tender and giving. Serve hot, with mashed potatoes.

Brined Christmas turkey

TECHNIQUE	Wet curing
CURING TIME	Minimum 24 hours

Roast turkey is a difficult thing to get right, what with the size, its tendency to dry out, and the bands of sinew and tendon in the legs. If you brine your turkey first, then it will remain moist and take on extra flavor. This is loosely based on a traditional Thanksgiving recipe.

Serves 6 to 8

1 free-range turkey, 10 to 12 lb
    (4.5 to 5.5 kg)

For the brine

5½ gallons water
5.5 lb (2.5 kg) PDV or other additive-
    free salt
2½ cups (1.1 lb/500 g) Demerara sugar
7 tbsp (2.1 oz/60 g) black peppercorns,
    cracked
2 heads garlic, halved horizontally

2 onions, sliced
A bunch of tarragon (with stalks)
A bunch of parsley (with stalks)
5 bay leaves
4 lemons, halved
1 (750 ml) bottle dry vermouth or gin
    (optional)

Equipment

Large food-grade brine tub
Meat thermometer

Place all of the ingredients for the brine, in a stockpot and bring to a boil, stirring often, to encourage the salt and sugar to dissolve. Remove from the heat and allow to cool completely; leave overnight if possible.

Put the turkey into a food-grade brine tub, pour in the brine, and place a plate or something similar on top to keep the turkey submerged. If you can get the tub in your fridge, do so. If not, put it in a cool place, such as a pantry. Keep your turkey in the brine for 24 to 36 hours. Remove the turkey from the brine, rinse it well under cold water, then pat dry. Let it rest, uncovered, in the fridge for at least 3 hours.

Cook the turkey as per your instructions. Alternatively, preheat the oven to 425°F and roast the turkey for 40 minutes (this initial blast is to get the heat right into the bird), then lower the oven setting to 325°F and cook for a further 3½ hours, until the internal temperature reaches 158°F. Check by placing a meat thermometer in the thickest part of a thigh. To be fancy, you could cure some of your own bacon and wrap the turkey breast in it.

Duck confit

TECHNIQUES	Dry curing, confit
CURING TIME	Minimum 3 days

Normally, curing relies on large quantities of salt; any fat present in the meat aids the curing process and enhances the flavor of the finished product. Here, the balance is tipped in the opposite direction. A large quantity of fat is used first to slowly cook the meat, creating a unique succulent texture, then as a preservative, forming a protective seal that stops oxygen and light from spoiling the meat.

Salt is used, too, but in the form of a very light cure that seasons more than it preserves. The preserved duck can be stored in the fridge for 6 months or more. When required, it is freed from its suspended animation in the solid fat and given a quick, hot blast of cooking that crisps the skin.

The best and most cost-effective way of making duck confit is to buy a whole duck. You can retrieve the fat from the carcass, then cut up the bird, using the legs for confit. The breasts can be hot smoked (see p. 226) or dry cured (see p. 183), and the rest of the carcass can be roasted and used to make stock.

There should be enough fat on the duck, when rendered, to cover both legs. If you don't want to buy a whole bird or there isn't enough fat, you can buy a carton of duck fat. Confit fat can be used several times until it becomes too salty.

Serves 2

1 large, whole duck (see above), or
    2 duck legs, about 7 oz (200 g) each,
    plus 1 lb (450 g) duck fat, lard,
    or a mixture of both (see above)

For the cure

About 7 oz (200 g) PDV or other
    additive-free salt (to cover the
    duck legs liberally)
A few sprigs thyme, lightly bruised
    (optional)
7 tsp (0.7 oz/20 g) black peppercorns,
    cracked (optional)

Equipment

Food-grade tray

(continued)

Duck confit, *continued*

If you are rendering the fat from a whole duck yourself, first pull all the fat away from the body, then cut up the duck. Put the fat into a heavy saucepan with about 3½ tablespoons water and place over very low heat. Leave it, uncovered, for several hours, until the fat has rendered down to a clear liquid.

Pass the liquid fat through a fine sieve into a bowl to remove any impurities. Place the duck legs on a food-grade tray.

Mix together the ingredients for the cure. This recipe requires a significant quantity of salt, equivalent to covering both of the duck legs. If you would like to store the legs in fat for anything more than a week, this amount will make the preservation more stable. Cover the duck legs all over with the cure and refrigerate overnight.

The following day, wash off the cure and pat the duck legs thoroughly dry, using a clean tea towel.

Preheat the oven to its lowest setting. Gently heat the fat you are using in a stockpot until it is liquid. Place the duck legs in the rendered fat, making sure they are completely covered. Put the stockpot over medium heat on the stove top. As soon as the fat begins to simmer, transfer the stockpot to the low oven and leave the duck legs to confit slowly: they will take between 8 and 10 hours to cook. When ready, they should be tender and submerged in clear fat. If you intend to cook the duck legs within a week, keep them in the stockpot and allow the fat to cool and set in the fridge.

If you want to store the duck legs for longer, transfer them to a container such as a sterilized widemouthed canning jar or earthenware pot. Pour the warm, liquid fat from the stockpot over them so they are completely submerged. Allow to cool then cover with plastic wrap before putting on the lid and refrigerating. Light can turn the fat rancid, so wrap the jar in aluminum foil to block it out completely. Leave the legs to mature for up to 6 months in the fridge. Their flavor will improve all the while.

To cook the legs, take the container from the fridge and leave it at room temperature for several hours to allow the fat to soften. Preheat the oven to 400°F. Remove the duck legs from the fat and place them in a roasting pan. Roast in the oven for 20 minutes, until the skin is crisp.

Sauerkraut

TECHNIQUES	Brining, fermentation
CURING TIME	2 weeks

This is a really simple brining and fermentation method for cabbage, giving it a tangy, bright lift while maintaining its fresh texture. Sauerkraut can be eaten raw, but it also benefits from being braised in a light stock, which reduces the acidity levels but none of the flavor. Cooked like this, it goes particularly well with the smoked ham hock terrine (p. 239). When brining vegetables, a ratio of 6 percent salt to liquid is perfect (see p. 112). Sauerkraut is a really great probiotic food.

Serves 10

1 red or green cabbage, about 2.2 lb
    (1 kg), thinly sliced or shredded

For the brine

4½ cups water
2.1 oz (60 g) PDV or other additive-
    free salt

Equipment

Large canning jar(s)

For the brine, put the water and salt in a large pot and bring to a simmer, stirring occasionally to encourage the salt to dissolve. Allow to cool, then chill the brine in the fridge to about 40°F.

Put the shredded cabbage into a bowl or plastic container and pour in the chilled brine so that it covers the cabbage. It is quite tricky to keep cabbage submerged in brine, but placing a sieve, the right way up, on top of the cabbage works well.

Cover the bowl (with the sieve still on top) with a tea towel or plastic wrap and leave in a cool place, such as a pantry, with an ambient temperature no higher than 74°F, for 2 weeks. This will allow fermentation to begin without letting harmful bacteria multiply.

After 2 weeks, drain the brine from the cabbage. Your sauerkraut is now ready to eat. You can either serve it as it is, in a similar fashion to coleslaw, or place it in a pan, cover it with chicken stock, and simmer it very gently for 30 minutes or so.

You can store the sauerkraut in a sealed large canning jar or large jars in the fridge for up to 3 weeks.

Hot smoked mackerel

TECHNIQUES	Dry curing, hot smoking
CURING & SMOKING TIME	16 minutes

I am fortunate to live and work within casting distance of Lyme Bay. When the mackerel are running, we clock off work with our fishing rods in hand and head off down to the shoreline. Our first job is to set a small driftwood fire going on the pebbled beach, and then it is time to tie feathers and a small ledger on the end of our lines, cast them out into the rushing waves, and spin them back to shore. It's a wonderful place to be if you don't catch a fish – and even better if you do.

Hot smoking mackerel fillets fresh from the sea is one of my favorite things to do. Lightly salted and cooked over oak sawdust, these are fantastic. They can also be used to make a tasty pâté – a great way to deal with a glut of shimmering fish.

Serves 4

4 mackerel, filleted

For smoking
Oak wood chips

For the cure
A generous pinch of sea salt per fillet
1 oz (30 g) dill, finely chopped (optional)

Equipment
Kitchen tweezers
Hot smoker

Check the mackerel fillets for pin bones and remove with tweezers. Add a pinch of the cure to the flesh side of each mackerel fillet (or just splash with seawater). After 8 minutes, wash off the cure (with seawater if you're on the beach) and pat dry. If you've used seawater to start with, just pat the fish dry.

Prepare the hot smoker with the oak wood chips (see pp. 118–22), place on the fire or other heat source, and smoke the mackerel fillets for 8 minutes. Eat immediately.

Hot smoked mackerel pâté

Skin 8.8 ounces (250 g) hot smoked mackerel fillet and put half in a food processor with 1 tablespoon each crème fraîche and lemon juice, 2 teaspoons freshly grated horseradish, and 1 teaspoon superfine sugar. Blend until smooth, then transfer to a bowl. Flake the remaining fish and stir the pâté with 1 teaspoon coarsely ground black pepper and a handful of dill or chives, finely chopped. Taste for seasoning and add more lemon juice, if necessary. Serve the pâté on buttered rye bread.

Hot smoked chicken
or pheasant breasts

TECHNIQUES	Dry curing, hot smoking
CURING & SMOKING TIME	32 to 35 minutes

This quick and easy recipe is a brilliant way to add flavor to poultry and game, and it keeps the meat lovely and moist. I have used the same cure on rabbit loins with great success.

Serves 4

4 organic chicken or pheasant breasts, skinned and boned

For the cure
¾ cup (5.2 oz/150 g) Demerara sugar
5.2 oz (150 g) PDV or other additive-free salt
1 tsp juniper berries, bruised
4 bay leaves, shredded
1 tsp black peppercorns, coarsely crushed

For smoking
Oak (or other) wood chips

Equipment
Food-grade tray
Hot smoker

Mix all of the cure ingredients together in a bowl.

Take a small plastic food-grade tray or something similar that is large enough to hold the chicken or pheasant breasts in a single layer. Scatter half the cure over the base of the tray, lay the breasts on the mixture, and scatter the remaining cure over the top of them.

Allow the meat to cure for just 12 to 15 minutes, then rinse the cure from the meat under a cold running tap and dry thoroughly with a tea towel. Store overnight in the fridge if you do not want to use them right away.

Prepare the hot smoker with the wood chips (see pp. 118–22), place on your heat source, and hot smoke the chicken breasts over gentle heat for 20 minutes, until they are cooked through. Allow to rest for 5 minutes before serving.

Smoked chicken (or pheasant) is delicious served cold with chutney, salad, and good bread.

Hot smoked rose-cured beef
with wood sorrel

| TECHNIQUES | Dry curing, hot smoking |
| CURING & SMOKING TIME | Minimum 14 hours |

There are times when it feels all the stars are aligned and everything is magically in place. The birth of this dish was one of them. Rarely have I been part of a food event as unique and stellar as the MAD Symposium in Denmark, inaugurated by René Redzepi, head chef of Noma. As part of this amazing trip, Hugh, Gill Meller, and I had the opportunity to cook for some of the best chefs in the world (including Ferran Adrià and Fergus Henderson, as well as René himself). With the help of some fantastic ingredients, Gill's confidence, and Hugh's direction and competitive edge, we put together one of the most memorable dishes I have ever been party to. This is a version of that dish. Do try it.

Serves 4

2.2 lb (1 kg) piece of aged beef sirloin, boned and trimmed

For smoking
Oak wood chips

For the cure
7 oz (200 g) fragrant rose petals
¼ cup (1.8 oz/50 g) superfine sugar
7 oz (200 g) coarse sea salt
1 tsp black peppercorns, coarsely crushed

Equipment
Food-grade tray
Hot smoker

For the dressing
½ cup (3.5 oz/100 g) superfine sugar
6½ tbsp water
3.5 oz (100 g) small alpine strawberries or sliced standard strawberries
3.5 oz (100 g) wild wood sorrel or common sorrel

Trim the sirloin of any extraneous fat. Put all of the cure ingredients into a bowl and mix together thoroughly, making sure you bruise the rose petals so they release their fragrance.

Select a food-grade tray large enough to hold the piece of beef. Scatter half the cure over the bottom of the tray, lay the sirloin on the mixture, and scatter the remaining cure over the top. Cover the tray and leave the meat to cure in a cool place for 1½ to 2 hours.

Rinse the cure off the beef under a cold running tap, then allow it to dry thoroughly – ideally overnight covered in the fridge.

Meanwhile, for the dressing, put the sugar, water, and strawberries in a pan over low heat and cook gently for about 5 minutes, until the berries have released their juices and you have a syrup. Let this cool, then strain and chill it.

Prepare the hot smoker with the wood chips (see pp. 118–22), place on your heat source, and hot smoke the sirloin for 30 minutes, until it is cooked to your liking. If you prefer, after 15 minutes, you can remove it from the smoker and sear it on a hot stove-top grill pan or outdoor grill (as we did in Denmark). This will give it a lighter smoke but with a caramelized thin crust. Allow the beef to rest for 5 minutes.

Thinly slice the cured beef onto a platter. Dress it with the strawberry syrup and garnish liberally with the wood sorrel. Serve to the great and the good – with a strong hint of pride.

Hot smoked pork tenderloin

TECHNIQUES	Dry curing, hot smoking
CURING & SMOKING TIME	Minimum 1¼ hours

When we get a whole pig carcass in the kitchen at River Cottage, the tenderloin is generally one of the first cuts we deal with. It does not lend itself to being frozen because it is so lean. Instead, we often whip it out, before any other major butchery takes place, dry cure it, and get it in the hot smoker.

Serves 4 to 6

1 free-range pork tenderloin

For smoking
Oak wood chips

For the cure

1 cup (7 oz/200 g) Demerara sugar
7 oz (200 g) PDV or other additive-free salt
5 bay leaves, shredded
20 juniper berries, bruised

Equipment
Food-grade tray
Hot smoker

Using a sharp knife, trim the tenderloin of any fat and silvery sinew.

Mix all of the cure ingredients together thoroughly in a bowl. Use the salt-box method to apply the cure to the tenderloin (see p. 98): place a handful of the cure in a small food-grade tray, sit the tenderloin on top, and completely cover with another handful of the cure. Now, either cover with a clean tea towel or place in the fridge for an hour, by which time the meat will have lost some moisture, which will be apparent in the cure around it, and be firmer and slightly darker in color.

Wash the cure from the tenderloin under a cold running tap and dry it thoroughly.

Prepare the hot smoker with the wood chips (see pp. 118–22), place on your heat source, and hot smoke the tenderloin for 10 to 12 minutes. Allow to rest for 4 minutes.

At this point, you could finish off the tenderloin by frying it in a little butter, but I would do that only if you aren't sure the internal temperature of the meat has reached at least 149°F. We like to serve the tenderloin slightly pink in the middle, which we can do with confidence, as the pork is of a high quality. It should be moist and melting, with a golden-brown, smoky exterior. Slice and serve – it makes a delicious canapé.

Pine-smoked mussels
with spinach

TECHNIQUE	Hot smoking
SMOKING TIME	5 to 8 minutes

Most of my favorite food experiences have been in the company of River Cottage pals, chief forager John Wright and head chef Gill Meller. They are not only good company but also generous with their knowledge. They taught me this way to cook mussels, which derives from a French technique, *éclade de moules*. The spectacle equals the taste, the burning pine needles imparting a fantastic flavor.

Serves 4

4.4 lb (2 kg) mussels
A knob of butter
1 tbsp olive oil
1 clove garlic, chopped
2 large handfuls of spinach
Sea salt and freshly ground black pepper

For smoking
A forager's basket full of very dry
   pine needles

Equipment
Kettle grill

Scrub the mussels well under a cold running tap and trim away the wiry beard from the side of the shell. Discard any mussels that are damaged or open (unless they close readily when you give them a sharp tap against the side of the sink).

Set a large metal tray outdoors supported on a flat surface, away from anything that could catch fire. It could be on a kettle grill or a bed of slate. Scatter a layer of pine needles over the tray. Lay the cleaned mussels, hinge side up and side by side, on top, then lay another stack of pine needles over the top, about 8 inches high.

Set fire to the pine needles in several places, all upwind of the tray, and give them a good blow to get them going. Once the pine needles have burned up (5 to 8 minutes), the mussels are ready to take out – carefully, as the shells can be hot.

Place a large pan over medium heat and add the butter, olive oil, and garlic. Cook for 1 minute, then add the spinach, cover, and cook for 2 to 3 minutes, until wilted. Add the pine-fired mussels in their shells, season with salt and pepper, and heat through. It's important to cook mussels properly, especially if you've foraged them yourself, although the heat from the pine needles should have done the trick. Serve at once.

Hot smoked oysters

TECHNIQUE	Hot smoking
SMOKING TIME	2 to 3 minutes

Oysters are fabulous on their own – freshly shucked and eaten raw. However, with a little bit of preparation and a light smoking, you can actually improve on the magic sensation of eating an oyster. Hot smoked for only a few minutes, they retain their fresh texture and taste sweet, smoky, and delicate. They are delicious just as they are, but I also love them with a little horseradish kick.

Serves 4 as a starter

12 oysters
2 tsp creamed horseradish
   (optional)

For smoking
Wood chips (of your choice)

Equipment
Kettle grill or hot smoker

Use either a kettle grill or hot smoker with your choice of wood chips (I like to use a combination of beech and ash). Have either the grill or smoker ready to place the wood chips in (see pp. 118–22).

Shuck the oysters with an oyster knife, taking care not to lose any of the liquor from the shells. Carefully release the oysters without removing them from their shells. The oysters will have been partially cured from the salt in the liquor.

Pour off a small amount of the liquor from a couple of the rounded bottom shells into a bowl and reserve to add to the horseradish, if using.

Put your wood chips into the embers of the grill or the hot smoker. Sit the oysters in their shells on the cooking grill of the smoker or grill and put the lid on. Cook and smoke for 2 to 3 minutes. In the meantime, mix the horseradish with the reserved liquor to loosen it and flavor it with a hint of the sea.

Lift out the oysters, using tongs since the shells will be quite hot, and place them, in their shells, on a serving board. Dab a little bit of horseradish on top of each one. Serve right away.

Smoked bream fillets
wrapped in prosciutto

TECHNIQUES	Dry curing, hot smoking
CURING & SMOKING TIME	25 to 30 minutes

My favorite white fish is sea bream, which smokes really well. The combination of the bream fillet with a thin protective layer of aged prosciutto ham and smoke shows all the best attributes of curing and smoking on a plate. It has the immediacy of a fresh smoked fish coupled with the aged majesty of a home-cured ham, and the textures are both melting and tender.

Serves 4

4 sea bream fillets, about 10.5 oz (300 g) each
8 slices prosciutto

For the cure
1¼ cups (8.8 oz/250 g) Demerara sugar
8.8 oz (250 g) PDV or other additive-free salt
A bunch of dill, chopped

For smoking
Wood chips (of your choice)

Equipment
Food-grade tray
Kettle grill or hot smoker

Have either the grill or hot smoker ready to place your chosen wood chips in (see pp. 118–22). Mix all of the cure ingredients together thoroughly in a bowl.

Put a small amount of the cure in a food-grade tray and place the bream fillets on top. Sprinkle more cure over the top of the fish so it has a liberal covering. Leave to cure in the fridge for just 15 minutes.

Rinse the fish under gently running cold water and then pat dry with a clean tea towel. Wrap the slices of prosciutto around the fish fillets. Put your wood chips into the embers of the grill or the hot smoker and smoke the wrapped bream fillets for 12 minutes, until cooked and lightly smoked. Serve with rye bread and salted butter and finish off with a splash of olive oil.

Variations
Other fish can be smoked in this way, such as pollack, salmon, or trout. You can also use small rosemary stems along with the wood chips for extra flavor.

Cedar-smoked duck breasts
with tea

TECHNIQUES	Dry curing, grill hot smoking
CURING & SMOKING TIME	40 to 45 minutes

I cook and smoke these duck breasts on the grill, and that is where the cedar comes in. I call it "wet grilling" because you soak the cedar plank in water before putting it into the hot grill to cook and smoke the duck. You will need a short, flat length of untreated wood or a small, nonprecious cutting board made from cedar or oak (not a pine plank, as this will create a bitter smoke), which fits inside your grill when the lid is on. You should soak this wood in water for a couple of hours prior to igniting the grill (or leave it out in a downpour!). If you don't have a length of cedar or other hardwood, you can still hot smoke the duck using any combination of wood chips.

Serves 2

2 duck breasts with skin, about 7 oz (200 g) each

For the cure

1¼ cups (8.8 oz/250 g) Demerara sugar
8.8 oz (250 g) PDV or other additive-free salt
7 tsp (0.7 oz/20 g) black peppercorns, freshly cracked
10 juniper berries

For smoking

Cedar plank or wood chips (of your choice)
A handful of loose black tea leaves, such as Earl Grey

Equipment

Food-grade tray
Kettle grill

Soak the cedar plank in cold water for 2 hours. Mix all the cure ingredients together thoroughly in a bowl.

Sprinkle a handful of the cure in a food-grade tray and place the duck breasts on top. Sprinkle another handful of cure over the duck so that it is gently dusted. Cover and leave to cure in the fridge for 30 minutes.

Heat up the grill. When it is ready (i.e., just as the coals are turning ash gray), place the sodden wooden board on top of the grill directly above the hot coals and put the lid on.

Rinse the duck breasts under cold running water to remove any of the remaining partially dissolved cure, then pat them dry with a clean tea towel. During this time, the wooden board will begin to crackle and gently smoke.

Put a handful of normal everyday dry tea leaves into the embers of the grill. This will create more smoke with a sweet aroma. Now place the duck breasts on top of the wooden board and replace the lid so that the smoke created envelops the duck breasts while the heat of the board cooks them through. The lid will also act as an umbrella should it be raining.

After 10 to 15 minutes, the duck breasts will be cooked to a nice, deep color and flavored with the exotic tea and wood smoke. They should also be wonderfully moist. Serve the smoked duck breasts with a summer salad.

Variation

Cedar-smoked Brie The cedar plank technique works really well for a whole Brie. You wouldn't normally hot smoke cheese, but placing the cheese on the plank in the grill for 5 minutes makes it deliciously soft with a mild smoky taste.

228 CURING & SMOKING

Oak-smoked spiced lamb

TECHNIQUES	Marinade, grill hot smoking
CURING & SMOKING TIME	Minimum 13 hours

If you own a kettle grill, you'll be able to smoke and roast large cuts of meat flavored with a marinade or rub and the sweet smokiness from whichever wood combination you choose. For this recipe I rub a *merguez* spice mix over a whole leg of lamb and let it infuse overnight before smoking the meat over charcoal.

Serves 6 to 8

A boneless leg of lamb, about 3.3 lb (1.5 kg), butterflied (flattened out)

For the rub

About 1 oz (30 g) PDV or other additive-free salt (i.e., 2 percent of the weight of the lamb)

2½ tbsp (0.7 oz/20 g) ground coriander
2½ tbsp (0.7 oz/20 g) ground cumin
2½ tbsp (0.7 oz/20 g) chile powder

7 tsp (0.7 oz/20 g) black peppercorns, freshly cracked
6 cloves garlic, chopped

For smoking

Wood chips (of your choice)

Equipment

Aluminum foil tray
Kettle grill

Mix together the ingredients for the rub and apply to the dried surface of the lamb leg with a gentle massage. Leave overnight in the refrigerator.

The following day, light your grill and nestle an aluminum foil tray, three-quarters full of water, next to the coals (see p. 129). Allow the coals to become gray and ashen as they get up to temperature. Remove the lamb from the fridge. The rub will have seasoned and salted the lamb, so that it will take on the wonderful flavors of the spices as well as the smoke from the grill.

Lay the lamb on the grill above the coals and cook for 15 minutes.

Now move the lamb to the other side of the grill so that it is directly above the foil water tray. Put a handful of wood chips on the charcoal and place the lid, with the vent open, on top. Cook and smoke for 30 minutes. Check to see if the charcoal or wood needs replenishing, then replace the lid. Cook and smoke for a further 15 minutes, then remove. Rest the lamb for 10 minutes before slicing and serving.

'Nduja
(Spreadable salami)

TECHNIQUES	Fermentation, cold smoking, air-drying
CURING & SMOKING TIME	Minimum 8 days

This is a traditional recipe from the south of Italy. To call it salami is almost a misnomer – it ought really to be described as a young, partially cured, smoked, partially dried, fresh meat salami spread. Unlike normal salami, *'nduja* is eaten only a week or so after making. Sliced out of its casing and spread on warm bruschetta, it's delicious.

Another difference from normal salami is that the meat tends to be the belly of pork rather than shoulder, so it is a little fattier. You could let the *'nduja* mature for 6 to 8 weeks to become fully dried salami, but that would mean missing out on the unique texture of meat and fat cured in this way.

Makes 15 to 20 small 'nduja

Hog (middle) casings

5.5 lb (2.5 kg) boneless free-range
pork belly, trimmed of rind

1.8 oz (50 g) PDV or other additive-
free salt (i.e., 2 percent of the total
weight of the meat)

Scant 2 cups (7 oz/200 g) smoked paprika
(either hot or sweet)

Scant ⅔ cup (1.8 oz/50 g) cayenne pepper

For smoking

Oak or other wood chips or sawdust

Equipment

Meat grinder

Sausage stuffer

Butcher's hooks and string

Cold smoker

Soak the hog casings overnight in cold water.

Prepare the meat grinder and sausage stuffer as described on p. 45. Grind the pork belly coarsely, using the ⅓-inch plate.

Put the ground pork into a large bowl and add the salt and spices. Mix together thoroughly until evenly combined.

Pack the mixture into the barrel of the sausage stuffer and fit a medium nozzle on the end. Load the casings onto the nozzle, and once you have pushed any air through and can see the salami mix in the nozzle, tie the end with string following

the method for tying salami described and illustrated on pp. 88–92. Fill the casing to create a 4- to 5-inch sausage and tie the other end with string.

Continue to fill the casings until you have used all of the mix. This should yield 15 to 20 small *'nduja* salami.

Use a sausage pricker or sterilized needle to release any air bubbles so that the skin shrinks back against the meat. Leave the *'nduja* salami to hang in a warm room at 79°F to 84°F for 12 to 24 hours to allow the fermentation process to begin and help incubate the desired bacteria.

Once the sausages have rested overnight, fire up your cold smoker and cold smoke the salami for 4 hours or so.

The salami should be air-dried for a week (see p. 103). They are then ready to split, spread, and eat. In the fridge, these salami will keep their moistness and spreadability for a further 4 weeks but will dry out and firm up like a normal salami beyond that time.

Pastrami

TECHNIQUES	Dry curing–brine hybrid, air-drying, cold smoking
CURING & SMOKING TIME	Minimum 10 days

This lovely deli staple has a unique texture – dry, lean, and almost flaky. The method takes in all the curing techniques: the beef is dry cured, wet cured, air-dried, then cold smoked. Unsurprisingly, it's one of my favorite recipes!

Makes 30 to 40 generous slices

6.6 lb (3 kg) joint of beef brisket or
    bottom round

1 tbsp ground ginger
2 tbsp coriander seeds, coarsely ground

For the cure

2.1 oz (60 g) PDV or other additive-
    free salt
5 cloves garlic, crushed
¼ cup brown sugar
¼ cup coarsely ground black pepper

For smoking

Oak or other wood chips or sawdust

Equipment

Food-grade tray
Butcher's hook
Cold smoker

Trim the meat of fat and put it into a large food-grade tray.

Mix the cure ingredients together and rub the mixture well into the meat. Cover and leave to cure in the fridge, allowing 1 day for every 2.2 pounds (1 kg), turning the meat every day. As moisture is drawn from the meat, the dry salt will become a wet brine. After the allotted time, remove the meat, rinse, and pat it dry with a clean tea towel.

Hang the meat in a cool, airy place for 5 days.

Now cold smoke the meat at a temperature below 86°F for 6 to 8 hours. Remove from the smoker and leave hanging in a cool, dry place for 24 hours.

Put the smoked meat in a large pan, add enough water to just cover, and bring to a simmer. Allow to simmer for 2 to 3 hours, until the meat is tender. Leave it to cool slightly in the liquid, then lift out. Put the meat into a dish, cover with a saucer, and put a weight on top to press down. Refrigerate overnight before slicing. The pastrami will keep for 4 to 6 weeks in the fridge. It's fantastic in sandwiches.

Hunter's sausage

TECHNIQUES	Fermentation, cold smoking, air-drying
CURING & SMOKING TIME	Minimum 4 weeks

Made using the salami method, pork and beef are ground through different plates for a rough-and-ready texture and livened up with spices. You don't have to be in the wild, rifle in hand, to enjoy this sausage – it's great in any lunch box.

Makes about 30 sausages

Hog (middle) casings
4.4 lb (2 kg) boneless shoulder or picnic
    shoulder of free-range pork
2.2 lb (1 kg) chuck steak or beef skirt
2.1 oz (60 g) PDV or other additive-
    free salt
tsp black peppercorns, freshly cracked
cloves garlic, minced
tsp mustard seeds, freshly ground
tsp garam masala
tsp ground ginger

For smoking
Oak or other wood chips or sawdust

Equipment
Meat grinder
Sausage stuffer
Cold smoker
Butcher's hooks and string

Soak the hog casings overnight in cold water.

Grind the pork and beef together through the large (⅓ to ⅜ inch) grinder plate, so that the grain is coarse. Pass about one-third of the mixture through the grinder a second time, using a smaller (¼ inch) plate. Combine the two different-textured meats with the salt, pepper, garlic, and spices, using your hands or a wooden spoon.

Pack the mixture into the sausage stuffer and fit a medium (¼ inch) nozzle on the end. Load the hog casings onto the nozzle. Following the method for tying salami described and illustrated on pp. 88–92, tie one end with string, then fill the casing to a length of 6 inches and tie the other end. Repeat to use all of the mixture.

Hang the sausages in a warm room (77°F to 81°F), making sure they're not touching one another, for 12 hours to allow fermentation and incubation of the desired bacteria to happen. After this time, the surface of the sausage will be dry to the touch.

Fire up your cold smoker and smoke the sausages for 4 to 6 hours. Then hang them to air-dry in the correct conditions (see p. 103). They should be ready in 4 weeks.

Pine-smoked merguez

TECHNIQUE	Cold smoking
CURING & SMOKING TIME	Minimum 20 hours

I love this spicy sausage, which combines two methods of dealing with lamb from very different origins. The classic, richly spiced *merguez* mix comes from Morocco, but the tradition of pine-smoking lamb sausages can be traced to the French town of Morteau near the border with Switzerland, an area thick with spruce and pine forests. It's a winning combination. These *merguez* are cooked, not eaten raw.

Makes 15 to 20 sausages

Sheep casings
2.2 lb (1 kg) boneless lamb shoulder
0.63 oz (18 g) PDV or other additive-
    free salt (for seasoning only)
2 cloves garlic, minced
1 tsp smoked paprika
1 tsp cayenne pepper
1 tsp black peppercorns, freshly cracked
½ tsp ground cumin
½ tsp ground allspice

For smoking
50-50 mix of pine and oak sawdust

Equipment
Meat grinder
Sausage stuffer
Cold smoker

Soak the sheep casings overnight in cold water.

Pass the lamb through the medium (¼ inch) plate of a grinder, then mix thoroughly in a bowl with all of the remaining ingredients. Pack the mix into the sausage stuffer and fit the smallest nozzle on the end. Load the sheep casings onto the nozzle and begin to fill. Sheep casings are smaller and have a greater tendency to break than others, particularly if they dry out on the nozzle or are even slightly overfilled. To combat this, keep dousing the loaded skins with cold water; any bagginess can be taken up by twisting them. Let the sausages dry naturally in the fridge overnight.

Put the pine and oak sawdust mix in the firebox of your cold smoker and smoke the sausages for 6 to 8 hours. They will now keep for 7 days in the fridge.

To cook the sausages, place in a cold frying pan and set over medium heat. They will release some of their lovely paprika-colored and -flavored fat, which becomes the cooking oil. The sausages will be cooked through and ready to eat in 20 minutes or so. Delicious served in flatbreads with a generous dollop of minted yogurt.

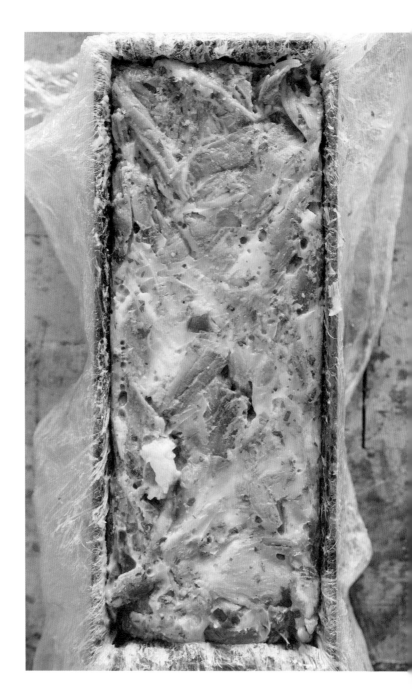

Smoked ham hock terrine

TECHNIQUES	Wet curing, air-drying, cold smoking
CURING & SMOKING TIME	5 to 6 days

A smoked ham hock is often referred to as a knuckle, and this recipe certainly packs a punch. A hock may be considered a lowly pork cut, but it makes a fantastic terrine.

Serves 6 to 8

2 ham hocks, 2.2 lb (1 kg) in total
A small bunch of flat-leaf parsley,
    leaves only, finely chopped

For the brine
3 qt cold water
4½ cups pressed apple juice
    (i.e., not from concentrate)
2.2 lb (1 kg) PDV or other additive-
    free salt
1 cup plus 2 tbsp (250 g) packed
    dark brown sugar
¼ cup (1.8 oz/50 g) Demerara sugar
5 bay leaves
2 star anise pods
1 cinnamon stick

For the stock
3 qt cold water
2 carrots, peeled
2 celery stalks
1 onion

For smoking
Oak (or other) wood chips or sawdust

Equipment
Food-grade brine tub
Butcher's hooks
Cold smoker

Put all of the brine ingredients in a large pot and bring to a boil, stirring to dissolve the salt and sugar. Let cool, then transfer to a brine tub. Add the ham hocks, put a plate on top to keep them submerged, and leave to cure in the fridge for 3 days (or the equivalent of 3 days per 2.2 pounds/1 kg). After the allotted time, remove the ham hocks and air-dry (see p. 103) for 2 days.

Now fire up your cold smoker and cold smoke the ham hocks for 4 hours.

Put the smoked hocks in a pan with the stock ingredients, bring to a simmer, and simmer gently for 3 hours. Turn off the heat and leave to cool. Lift out the hocks. Remove and shred the meat, discarding the skin. Strain the stock into another pan and boil to reduce. Line a terrine with plastic wrap. Mix the meat with the parsley, pack into the terrine, and pour in stock to cover. Let the terrine cool, then refrigerate overnight or until set. Turn out onto a board and slice.

Cold smoked pollack
with poached egg

TECHNIQUES	Dry curing, cold smoking
CURING & SMOKING TIME	Minimum 6 hours

This simple recipe shows how a gentle lick of smoke across a wonderful fillet of fish can have an immense impact. It also reminds me of some of my favorite people, the Fisher family. That kinship is not only because we share the synchronicity of a surname related to our passions but also because I know that Nick Fisher serves this dish to his wife, Helen, as an antidote to the stresses of the day, which just about sums up the practice of cold smoking perfectly. If you have any left over, flakes of smoked pollack are lovely added to the potato salad on p. 244.

Serves 2

2 pollack fillets, about 14 oz (400 g) each

For the cure

**2.6 oz (75 g) PDV or other additive-
  free salt**

**⅓ cup (2.6 oz/75 g) packed light
  brown sugar**

3½ tbsp (0.7 oz/20 g) fennel seeds

To serve

A bay leaf

3 to 5 black peppercorns

2 cups whole milk

2 tbsp cider vinegar

2 extra-large very fresh organic eggs

For smoking

50-50 mix of beech and oak sawdust

Equipment

Food-grade tray

Cold smoker

Butcher's hooks

Mix all of the cure ingredients together in a bowl and then sprinkle a couple of handfuls (or at least half of the mix) in a food-grade tray. Place the pollack fillets, skin side down, on the cure mix and then cover them liberally with the rest of the cure. Leave to cure in the fridge for at least 2 hours and no longer than 4 hours. (After this time, the pollack flesh will lose its plump flakiness and become too dehydrated.)

(continued)

Cold smoked pollack, *continued*

After the allotted time, wash the residual cure from the fish under cold running water and then pat dry with a clean tea towel. Put the beech and oak sawdust in your firebox and either place your fillets on racks or hang them from butcher's hooks inside the smoking chamber. Occasionally, if you hang them like this, the fillets dry out around the hooks, causing the flesh to rip, and the fillets drop off the hook. Placing them flesh side down on a rack prevents this, but you do sometimes get a crosshatch pattern of the rack on the flesh that I don't actually mind. To avoid this, you can tie string around the tail end of the fillet using a butcher's knot (see pp. 148–49) and hang them up.

Depending on how smoky you like your pollack, you should cold smoke it for anywhere from 4 to 8 hours.

After smoking, place the fillets in a large saucepan in a single layer, cutting them in half to fit if necessary. Add the bay leaf and peppercorns and cover with the milk. Put the lid on and place over medium heat until the liquid starts to simmer, then take off the heat. Leave covered for a couple of minutes to allow the fish to cook through in the residual heat.

Meanwhile, bring a small saucepan of water to a boil, add the vinegar, and create a small whirlpool in the water by stirring with a spoon. Now carefully crack the eggs into the vortex. Turn the heat down to the minimum and cook the eggs for about 3 minutes. The whites should set around the central yolks like newly formed planets.

When the smoked pollack is cooked, remove it from the liquid and plate it. Using a slotted spoon, remove the poached eggs from the pan, allowing any water to drain off, then place on top of the smoked pollack.

Oak-smoked Cheddar

TECHNIQUE	Cold smoking
SMOKING TIME	Minimum 4 hours

I usually cold smoke cheese as an extra product alongside something else, like a salami or side of bacon. It's incredibly simple and requires no curing or drying. You just slip your cheese into the cold smoker along with your other goodies, and it will emerge, invitingly tanned and earthy, after its gentle, smoky immersion.

Hard cheeses, such as Cheddar, work best and absorb more flavor if their rind is removed first. Place a large piece of cheese, about 1.7 pounds (800 g) in weight, on a rack in the cold smoker for 4 to 6 hours and then enjoy. As with all cold smoking, the temperature of the smoke chamber should not exceed 86°F. Spices or herbs can be added before smoking – try dusting Cheddar lightly with paprika.

You can experiment with smoking materials, too. A traditional Danish cheese is smoked with fresh hay and nettles. The hay is lit, then damped down with nettles to create a thick smoke, which envelops the cheese. It is ready in about an hour.

Smoked new potato salad

TECHNIQUE	Cold smoking
SMOKING TIME	Minimum 1 hour

I like to use new potatoes for this salad. As with anything you smoke, their surface must be dry before you put them in the smoker, or the smoke particles will only attach themselves to the moisture on the outside rather than creating a pellicle, or smoky skin, on the surface.

Serves 6 to 8

2.2 lb (1 kg) new potatoes
1 red onion, finely chopped, or
   3 green onions, sliced
A handful of herbs, such as snipped
   chives or young rosemary sprigs

For smoking
Oak (or other) wood chips or sawdust

Equipment
Cold smoker

For the vinaigrette
1 tsp coarse sea salt
1 clove garlic, chopped
2 tsp balsamic vinegar

Put the potatoes in a saucepan, add just enough water to cover them, bring to a boil, and simmer for 15 minutes, until just tender. Drain them in a colander and allow them to cool and dry.

Peel the potatoes and place them in the cold smoker for just about an hour or so. Leave to cool.

For the vinaigrette, shake the ingredients together in a screw-top jar to emulsify. Taste and adjust the seasoning.

Toss the cold smoked potatoes with the onion and the vinaigrette dressing. Scatter the herbs over the top and serve.

Variations

At the same time as cold smoking the potatoes, you could place a few peeled, hard-boiled eggs in the cold smoker, then chop them and add to the salad. You could even cold smoke the oil for the dressing to enhance the smoky effect.

Useful Things

Notes to the US Edition

In editing this book for an American audience, we sought to do two things: (1) to make it as much a treasure trove of information and inspiration for Americans as it is for its original British audience; and (2) to retain Steven Lamb's engaging style. To that end, the recipes, as well as the information about ingredients and equipment, have been Americanized as fully as possible, so that the ingredients, terminology, and measurements are familiar to US readers. We've made our best attempt to address these particulars. Any errors or omissions are those of the American publisher, Ten Speed Press.

Measurements In the recipes and instructional text, weight and volume measurements (both US and metric units for weights) are included for dry ingredients when possible. This is because volume measurements are regularly used in the United States for many dry ingredients, such as sugar. Salt is the exception here, as different types of salt measure differently by volume, and an accurate measurement, which is possible only by weight, is critical to a successful result (see p. 83). Measurements for liquid ingredients are expressed in US units only.

Equipment A jambon sac (sac à jambon), which is used for hanging meat for air-drying, is a 100 percent cotton bag that is large enough to allow for good air circulation and lightweight enough to visually monitor the meat's condition. If you cannot locate one, a blousy bag fashioned from cheesecloth or muslin can be used in its place.

For specialized-equipment needs discussed in the text, from a meat grinder to butcher hooks to a brinometer, search out a shop selling high-quality butcher supplies in your area or check for sources online.

PDV salt The recipes call for PDV (pure dried vacuum) salt (see pp. 82–83). Any additive-free salt, such as most kosher salt, can be used in its place.

Brine table The table on p. 113, which provides gram and milliliter measurements for brines of various salinity strengths, has not been converted to US units of measurement because equivalent ounce and fluid-ounce amounts, the latter of which are less precise, would not yield the same salinity percentages. As pointed out on p. 112, the precision reflected in this table is not necessary to successful brining. The best way to measure the salinity of your brines is with a brinometer (see p. 52).

Acknowledgments

My role at River Cottage is varied and fun. It comes with some responsibilities. I teach, write, mess about in front of the camera, and often find myself at serious gatherings around the world talking about what River Cottage stands for. Surrounded by experts and mavericks, I absorb everything like a sponge. I have been at River Cottage from the beginning. It has been the best apprenticeship possible and has afforded me the best job in the world – a job that has enabled me to find subjects I am passionate about and ultimately lead me to write this book. There are a few people I would like to sincerely thank for this:

Ray Smith was my teacher. Learning at the shoulder of Ray was such a wonderful experience. I hope this book proves I was a worthy student.

Hugh is a friend and an inspiration. Hugh, we do what we do on your behalf and in your name. What an amazing opportunity you have given us all.

I have worked with Rob Love longer than anyone I know, and he leads from the front with immense drive and vision.

Gill Meller is a legend. Most of my best food moments have had Gill at the center of them. His team of chefs and KPs are second to none. Their support in putting the recipes together in this book has been immense.

Mark Diacono and John Wright share equal parts of humor, expertise, and generosity of spirit. They have many books each under their belts but willingly gave advice and showed a genuine interest in helping me put this together.

Natalie Hunt and Xa Shaw Stewart at Bloomsbury are the dream team. A pleasure to work with, they add in a whole lot of guidance, direction, patience, and fun. Thanks also to Marina Asenjo and Alison Glossop at Bloomsbury for their roles.

Nikki Duffy has been a tremendous asset. It is a pleasure to work with you, Nikki.

Gavin Kingcombe's photos are art. What a joy he is to collaborate with.

Janet Illsley has the eye of an eagle for detail, and Will Webb's design is exemplary.

Chris Moorsby, head of butchery and charcuterie at Leeds City College, and Peter R. Sherratt of the Salt Association, thank you for your scientific checks.

My darling Elli, thanks for your love, support, and encouragement, and for our two incredible little girls, Aggie and Betsy, who often sat on my lap while I was writing this book.

And, of course, thanks to my parents.

Index

Other handbooks from River Cottage

The River Cottage Booze Handbook
$22.00
ISBN: 978-1-60774-785-7
eBook ISBN: 978-1-60774-786-4

The River Cottage Preserves Handbook
$22.00
ISBN: 978-1-58008-172-6
eBook ISBN: 978-1-60774-082-7

The River Cottage Bread Handbook
$22.00
ISBN: 978-1-58008-186-3
eBook ISBN: 978-1-60774-083-4